FORENSIC PSYCHIATRY IN ISLAMIC JURISPRUDENCE

Forensic Psychiatry in Islamic Jurisprudence

Kutaiba S. Chaleby

THE INTERNATIONAL INSTITUTE OF ISLAMIC THOUGHT

THE INTERNATIONAL INSTITUTE OF ISLAMIC THOUGHT
P.O. BOX 669, HERNDON, VA 22070, USA

LONDON OFFICE
P.O. BOX 126, RICHMOND, SURREY TW9 2UD, UK

ISBN 1-56564-276-7 paperback
ISBN 1-56564-277-5 hardback

Typesetting by Sohail Nakhooda
Cover Design by Shiraz Khan
Printed in the United Kingdom
by Biddles Limited, Guildford and King's Lynn

CONTENTS

FOREWORD

Of knowledge, we have none, save what
You have taught us. (The Qur'an 2:32)

The International Institute of Islamic Thought (IIIT) is pleased to present this pioneering work which explores new ideas and thoughts in the field of forensic psychiatry from an Islamic perspective. The author, Dr. Kutaiba S. Chaleby, specialises in forensic psychiatry and has a wide and extensive knowledge of the subject-area which he combines with accessibility to the Shariʿah. His long experience at psychiatric centres (especially fourteen years as head of the section of Psychiatry at King Faisal Hospital), together with the various teaching posts he has held in both Muslim and non-Muslim countries including Louisiana University in the States and his work at a number of centers and hospitals in the West, has provided him with the necessary tools to demonstrate how contemporary forensic psychiatry relates to Shariʿah. He successfully shows that some of the major issues and concerns of forensic psychiatry have already been tackled with a great deal of sophistication and precision by Muslim scholars in the past.

Indeed this is the first book in the field of forensic psychiatry which seeks to focus on the application of psychiatry to legal issues connected with Islamic Jurisprudence. Holding a unique position amongst the world's religions in its containment of every aspect of human existence, it is openly natural for Islam to govern both the spiritual and legislative aspects of life. It is therefore not surprising that one of the most important conclusions drawn by the study is the ability of Islamic jurisprudence to cover almost every issue raised in the field of forensic psychiatry. The range of interpretations encompassing these issues is so wide that a match for many aspects of different secular laws can be found in at least one of the four schools of thought. This gives contemporary psychiatry in any Islamic country a broad spectrum of tools to work with, enabling the utilisation of options specific to particular societal and cultural norms. This book will appeal to both the general as well as the academic reader drawing important and wide-ranging conclusions relevant for many individuals and societies in the Islamic world.

Forensic Psychiatry, like other pioneering works published by the IIIT, will not only make an important contribution to the field of the Islamization of the behavioral sciences, but will hopefully generate much interest among specialists to analyze and further develop the ideas and theories presented and discussed.

The IIIT, established in 1981, has served as a major center to facilitate sincere and serious scholarly efforts based on Islamic vision, values and principles. Its programs of research, seminars and conferences during the last twenty years have resulted in the publication of more than two hundred and sixty titles in English and Arabic, many of which have been translated into several other languages.

We would like to express our thanks and gratitude to Dr. Chaleby, who, throughout the various stages of the book's production, cooperated closely with the editorial group at the IIIT London Office. He was very helpful in responding to our various queries, suggestions and amendments.

We would also like to thank the editorial and production team at the London Office and those who were directly or indirectly involved in the completion of this book: Dr. Jamil Qureishi, Sohail Nakhooda, Shiraz Khan, Ataiya Pathan and Dr. Maryam Mahmood. May God reward them and the author for all their efforts.

Rabiᶜ al-Awwal 1422
July 2001

ANAS AL-SHAIKH-ALI
Academic Advisor
IIIT London Office, UK

AUTHOR'S INTRODUCTION

ABOUT THIS BOOK

The history of forensic psychiatry as a sub-discipline of psychiatry (itself a speciality within medicine) is a subject that needs separate attention which cannot be attempted here. For our purposes it suffices to accept the current definition as adopted by the American Board of Forensic Psychiatry and by the American Academy of Psychiatry and Law:

> Forensic psychiatry is a sub-specialty of psychiatry in which scientific and clinical expertise is applied to legal issues in legal contexts embracing civil, criminal, correctional or legislative matters; forensic psychiatry should be practiced in accordance with guidelines and ethical principles enunciated by the profession of psychiatry.[1]

That definition has replaced and expanded on the older, more popular perception which limited forensic psychiatry to psychiatric evaluations for legal purposes.

The importance of forensic psychiatry does not end in the fact that it encompasses the overlap between law and medicine, two major fields of knowledge in human life. In fact, it touches on issues that affect both the individual and society as a whole through its direct involvement in criminal, civil and, most important, family law. The number of individual psychiatric–legal issues is therefore vast and, moreover, for each such issue, there is a variety of legal contexts in which it may arise. 'Legal context' is itself variable with the multiplicity of jurisdictions and legal traditions and criteria. Our aim, in this book, is to present a preliminary study of issues that fall within the domain of forensic psychiatry in one particular legal context, namely Islamic law. But what is 'Islamic law'?

The practical answer to this question should be: "the law as it is in one or other Islamic country." But the matter is not so straightforward. The present legal system in many Islamic countries has in part been derived, as a direct result of the rule of foreign colonial powers, from the French or English or other European legal traditions, themselves evolved from the ancient Roman law. However, in matters of personal status, family relationships and inheritance, almost all Islamic countries retained the Shariʿah or Islamic law proper. In recent decades particularly, the aspiration to cultural as well as political independence, and among Muslims, a renewed interest in Islam, has induced a strong and popular demand to adopt the Islamic Shariʿah as the main, and even, in some countries, the only, source of legislation.

My interest in the subject derives from fifteen years of service as chairman of the Psychiatric Consulting Committee of the Ministry of Health in Saudi Arabia. The Committee encountered many legal issues related to the actions of people who were mentally ill, or who were alleged or claimed to be mentally ill. Also, we have had to meet the challenges of shaping mental health policy to regulate (among other things) involuntary hospitalization and the legal rights of the mentally ill. It was our duty to advise on legal decisions so as to com-ply with the religious and cultural traditions of the country, which means the religion and traditions of Islam. The need to evolve what we may call an 'Islamic forensic psychiatry' was a practical one. I was encouraged to develop basic guidelines for psychiatrists to help them treat patients or make decisions on forensic issues in ways that are Islamically oriented and Islamically acceptable. A draft of the work proposed was presented in 1986 to Shaykh Ibn Bāz, Head of the Fatwa Assembly in Saudi Arabia, who reviewed it and urged me to continue with it. It took several years of study to produce a general text on forensic psychiatry that included some of the Islamic legal views on the subject. That text was completed with the help of Shaykh Ṣāliḥ al-Leḥaidān, consultant and chief judge in the Ministry of Justice, and published in Arabic in Cairo in 1996.

The next step was to write a text devoted directly to the relevance of Islamic Shariʿah to the work of forensic psychiatrists. It began with a presentation in 1993, at the annual meeting of the American Academy of Psychiatry and Law, on the Islamic view of legal issues in psychiatry. So many prominent figures in the field were kind enough to express interest in the paper that I was encouraged to publish it, after further research, in the *Bulletin of the Academy of Psychiatry and the Law* under the title 'Forensic Psychiatry in Islamic Law' (1996). Following its publication, I received many communications from psychiatrists in Islamic and non-Islamic countries stressing the need for a longer study that could guide them in their practice, and contribute to the drafting of mental health legislation rooted in the spirit and the purposes of Islamic Shariʿah.

That there is a need for mental health legislation, and for guidance for the practice of forensic psychiatry, in Islamic contexts is, I am sure, widely recognized. 'In Islamic contexts' does not have to mean 'within Islamic jurisdictions': there are Muslims living in large numbers under non-Islamic jurisdiction who nevertheless share the same need. I hope that this book will demonstrate that the need can be met from within the resources of the Shariʿah itself. Those who come to the subject for the first time will be amazed by the sheer depth of those resources: the great scholars of *fiqh* (jurisprudence) to whose work we shall be referring were extraordinarily far-sighted, profoundly humane, compassionate and flexible in their understanding of how to apply the law of Islam. There is much that we can learn from them to inspire and guide our practice in the present day. While I have no interest in seeking to vindicate the Islamic tradition over against any other, it would be a kind of intellectual dishonesty not to acknowledge the fact that Islamic scholars were able to make subtle and sophisticated distinctions between kinds and degrees of mental illness, and their consequences for the definition of legal competence and responsibility, that do not appear in the Western secular tradition until the modern period.

This work, it bears repeating, is oriented to the practical needs of practitioners in the field. Therefore, as the chapter titles indicate, the work is arranged around particular practical issues. The book is not a 'historical study' such as would aim to narrate the development of ideas, epoch by epoch and school by school, in a chronological sequence. Our aim, in this first book-length study of the subject, is to show how the resources available in the tradition of Islamic *fiqh* can help us to resolve the difficulties we encounter, on a daily basis, as we deal with individual legal–psychiatric issues. To serve that purpose the authorities to which we refer – for examples of legal reasoning or legal rulings (precedents) – needed to be the most widely respected figures, scholars of recognized juristic stature, in the history of Islamic law. (In a different context it might be of interest to reflect upon the exceptional or wayward thinkers of the past, but not here.) We have added, in the Appendix, a series of case-examples that were presented to a practising judge of established authority for his counsel and opinion. The aim was to give concrete, practical form to some of the matters discussed at a (necessarily) more theoretical level in the main part of the book, and to bring out more clearly some of the nuances in that discussion.

Readers will note that, on certain matters of Islamic law, we judged it appropriate and worthwhile to elaborate more fully than the specialized focus of forensic psychiatry itself would appear to justify. We believe that, for these matters, forensic psychiatrists need to understand the Islamic legal context well enough to be able to relate their expertise to it effectively. For example, a psychiatrist must understand the restricted legal power of an individual's will to undo a natural heir's right of inheritance – especially if the intent in making the will was precisely to disinherit the heir – before he or she can determine the mental competence of the individual at the time of making the will or his intentions in so doing.

As we could not assume that all readers of this book will be equally or sufficiently familiar with the special characteristics of Islamic law, we have devoted the remainder of this introduction to a brief overview. This overview does not, to our knowledge, make any controversial or otherwise remarkable statement; it merely puts down as concisely as possible generally uncontested facts. Readers who need no introduction to Islamic law may turn directly to the next chapter.

ABOUT THE SHARIʿAH OR ISLAMIC LAW

The way the Shariʿah operates in practice is not very different from the way that (for example) Anglo-American law operates in practice. There is a body of texts (the 'written law') which are subject to interpretation by lawyers and judges; the interpretation is not arbitrary – it must proceed according to the rules and standards of the legal profession; there are various levels of courts and judges dealing with different kinds of matters according to their gravity or complexity; and there are established procedures of referral (appeal) from one level to a higher one. However, Islamic law is unique in that its body of texts (called *naṣṣ*) are of divine rather than human origin. Laws made by man (whether decreed by a monarch or a tribal chief, or by a body of priests or by a legislature of elected representatives of the 'sovereign will of the people') are subject to the influences of time and place, the pressure of individuals or interest-groups, public mood, and other factors. Therefore, such laws can change over time: what one generation regards as a heinous immoral act and so designates a crime may, in the next generation, become morally acceptable and is then neither regarded nor punished as a crime. Some parts of the law in man-made legal systems may change very slowly compared to others – constitutional law, for example, in politically stable countries, hardly changes at all over the generations – but, in principle, all parts of the law are subject to modification.

That is not the case with Islamic law. Important and substantial parts of the Shariʿah are fixed in the *naṣṣ* and can never be modified. Exceptions or exemptions are only countenanced to the degree that they are expressly sanctioned in the *naṣṣ*. For example, among the dietary laws of Islam, the consumption of pork is *ḥarām* (forbidden) by the Qur'an; the exemption for that is also in the Qur'an: in extreme situations of dire necessity, in order to preserve human life, provided no other food is available and provided the person is not desirous of breaking the law, pork becomes *ḥalāl* (lawful) for the duration of the necessity. Further interpretation of this exemption is the task and responsibility of qualified scholars. Some scholars may rule that this exemption allows (again, only in order to save human life, and again, no substitute being available) that some part or other of a pig may be used, for example, in a life-saving drug or other medical treatment. Such an interpretation would be subject to further amendment or contradiction by another qualified scholar, or by a change in circumstance (for example the availability of a substitute): but the particular prohibition and the particular exemption as these stand in the Qur'an stand for all time.

The *naṣṣ* upon which the Shariʿah is founded comprise, first and foremost, the *aḥkām* of the Qur'an (those verses, about 500 in all, that are explicit commands), and, secondarily, the rulings, precepts and practice of the Prophet (ṢAAS)[1] as recorded in the Hadith. The authority of the Hadith (the record of what the Prophet said and did) is conferred by the Qur'an (4:59): it commands believers to obey the Prophet and those among the society of Muslims who have authority over them, and to refer any matters of dispute to the judgment of the Prophet (and, self-evidently, that of the persons he appointed to positions of authority). In the formative period of Islam, those in authority among the Muslims were appointed on account of their learning and piety so that there was no formal distinction between legal and political authority. Over time, there was a measure of specialization, and the duty of understanding and interpreting the law was discharged by learned scholars whose authority in Islamic society (always very considerable, virtually until the colonial period) was distinct from the authority of those who wielded executive power.

The commands of the Qur'an have always been beyond dispute. Some of the *aḥkām* are particular and some are general commands, but they do not cover every circumstance nor every eventuality. To be able to do that, Islamic scholars had to exercise conscience and reason (ijtihad): to infer the general principles behind the particular commands so as to apply them appropriately in different or new circumstances; and to understand the intent of the general commands so as to apply them appropriately as laws rather than ethical principles. In the same way, the texts in the Hadith required interpretive effort. The great Ḥanbalī jurist, Ibn Qayyim al-Jawziyyah, gives a particularly clear example.[2] For the duration of a fast, as well as eating and drinking, sexual intercourse is forbidden. The Prophet instructed a young man not to indulge in any physical intimacy with his wife during the period of the fast, but permitted the same to an old man. The reasoning behind this was that the old man was more likely to be able to restrain himself from going on to do that which is forbidden during the fast. Another example: one year the Prophet ordered the people to distribute all the meat of their sacrifices by the third day without allowing it to be stored; in another year, he asked them to store whatever they could.[3] The reason for the latter ruling was that, in that year, there was great scarcity of food. This kind of flexibility in the judgments of the Prophet showed that it is necessary, in order to effect the purposes of the law in different circumstances, to devise appropriate rulings which hold until the circumstances change.

The effort to understand the Qur'an and Hadith as law is called *fiqh* or jurisprudence. The *aḥkām* of the Qur'an, as we have noted, were always beyond dispute. The texts of the Hadith, by contrast, were not all as uniform or as stable as the Qur'an. Dedicated scholars anxious to serve the cause of Islam travelled great distances between centers of learning in order to acquire and exchange knowledge of Hadith. Nevertheless, some Hadith texts became well-known in one region but did not gain the same recognition or currency in another. Also, scholars could not always agree on the legal weight of certain texts compared to others. Some of the texts were based upon a large number of reports conveyed through many lines of transmission by narrators of impeccable trustworthiness and excellent memory. Such texts clearly reflected the normative practice of the Prophet or 'Sunnah'. However, other texts were reported only by a single narrator and referred to a single remembered incident, and their wording and their intent could not be so easily or reliably cross-checked against other texts received through different lines of transmission.

Over time, patterns of interpretive effort or *fiqh* developed and settled as 'schools' of Islamic law. It would be a grave misconception to suppose that there was serious division on any important matter between the 'schools'. Differences were over relatively minor detail, and generally derived not from any disagreement of principle, but from the fact that the *fiqh* (the legal reasoning) was done using different Hadith texts, or giving a different legal weight to the same texts.

The great jurists regularly made reference to the reasoning and dicta of schools other than the one in which they had been trained, and used the same to evolve the *fiqh* of their own school. Naturally, both for the purposes of training lawyers and judges, and to achieve administrative uniformity within jurisdictions, the *fiqh* of one school rather than another came to predominate in a particular region. But the variety of judgments available was valued as a blessing for the Muslims as a whole, and to hold (what people nowadays would call) 'a minority view' was never considered a transgression. For several hundred years now, the overwhelming majority of Muslims have accepted the authority of four schools of Islamic law: the Mālikī, the Shāfiʿī, the Ḥanbalī, and the Ḥanafī.

It is most important to appreciate that Islamic law evolved as an autonomous institution, independent of the state or political power. Laws or regulations issued by the state did not have the moral or legal authority of the Shariʿah. Such law codes were called *qānūn* (related to the English 'canon') and could be promulgated to regulate narrowly defined domains of activity or transaction (for example, the administration of traffic or hospitals or agrarian practice, or the regime of standards for particular professions) provided there was no contradiction with the Shariʿah. In principle, the Shariʿah is comprehensive of all departments of collective life: the rites of worship; family relationships (marriage, divorce, custody of children, inheritance); civil and commercial transactions; crime and punishment; certain taxes and expenditure therefrom; charitable endowments; inter-communal relations between Muslims and non-Muslims; government and administration; international treaties and obligations; and so on. The Shariʿah is not a religious law in the limited Western sense of a law that regulates the properties or bureaucracy of the church or its powers to define rites and services or discipline its officers. When we affirm that no state regulation may contradict the Shariʿah, we affirm the potential of the Shariʿah to function as a strong, positive restraint on the power of the state, as indeed it did function in varying degrees throughout the pre-modern period of Islamic history; we do not merely express a wish that it ought to or might be so.

THE PRINCIPLES OR SOURCES OF *FIQH*

The exercise of ijtihad, which we defined as the exercise of conscience and reason by qualified scholars to understand the *naṣṣ* as law, was not arbitrary. It was guided by the general maxim – to encourage and promote the good and to discourage and prevent the harmful. Under that general maxim, which we will describe separately, ijtihad followed clearly defined and understood principles or *uṣūl al-fiqh* which functioned, after the *naṣṣ*, as sources of law.

1. *Juristic Consensus* (*ijmāʿ*)

When all Islamic scholars agree on a particular issue, that agreement is accepted as Islamic law. The consensus of the scholars may take either of two forms. One is the explicit consensus such as when the scholars actually meet and discuss the matter and agree on a particular ruling, or when a particular decision is made by a scholar with which other scholars in different parts of the world at that time are in agreement. The second is an implicit consensus, as when one scholar gives a ruling on an issue and no objection to it is raised or announced.

2. *Analogy* (*qiyās*)

On matters for which there is no explicit ruling in the Qur'an and Hadith sources, laws could be made by analogy, where one particular ruling is based on another that has some circumstantial similarities. For example, Islamic law expressly forbids wine because it is an intoxicating drink. The rule was extended by analogy to include all intoxicating drugs. There are some problems in using analogy as it is usually based on the underlying attributes of the Qur'anic ruling. It is easy in the matter of prohibiting alcohol because it is clear that alcohol causes alteration of consciousness; therefore, other kinds of drugs that do the same can be defined as forbidden on the same principle. However, the underlying attributes of some of the *aḥkām* are not made explicit in the Qur'an, and therefore it requires very wide knowledge and understanding of the Hadith, of the Sunnah of the Prophet and of the practice of his Companions and their successors, to be able to infer the rationale with sufficient reliability to permit analogous rulings to be made. Certainly, it is a most onerous task for which only the most learned scholars are qualified.

3. *Juristic Preference* (*istiḥsān*)

When a rule derived by *qiyās* is not well defined or if it has been decided upon the basis of a precedent that is contradicted by a *qiyās* which yielded a different ruling, the jurist is faced with a choice. *Istiḥsān* refers to the preference between two analogies.

4. *Public Interest* (*al-maṣāliḥ al-mursalah*)

Assuming always that there was no contradiction of the intent of the primary sources of the law (the *naṣṣ*), scholars could, on matters on which the *naṣṣ* were silent, issue rulings that served the well-being of the society. Well-being was never understood in the narrow sense of economic prosperity, though that was important and relevant, but embraced the Islamic ethos of society as a whole and such factors as would concern the Muslims' security, cohesion and solidarity.

5. *Local Social Norms and Customs* (*ʿurf*)

This is a regular principle in almost all legal systems. Islamic *fiqh* recognizes the legal force of local customs and practice insofar as there is no contradiction between these and the two primary sources of Islamic law proper, the Qur'an and the normative practice of the Prophet, the Sunnah. Local customs and practice do not cover only habits of dress or language, but also ways of doing business, of celebrating important occasions, and so on. Over time certain norms come to function as expected standards for a particular service or profession without necessarily being explicitly stated in legal terms. Similarly, certain kinds of commercial transaction are done on the basis of mutual understanding of terms that are not necessarily written out. In this way, local customs and practice set up implied contracts which, provided there was no contradiction with Islamic law proper, were recognized in Islamic courts: if one party to such an implied contract had not fulfilled conditions affirmed by the relevant social norms for the particular transaction, the judge would rule accordingly. The basis for the acceptance of local customs and practice is Qur'an and Sunnah: some of the pre-Islamic practices of the Arabs were approved and some annulled by the Qur'an; similarly, the Prophet accepted some of the inherited ways of doing things, forbade or altered others.

6. *The 'Law Before Ours'* (*shara*ᶜ *ma qablana*)

Islamic jurisprudence recognized a decision based on what had been legislated for Jews and Christians in their Scriptures provided that such law was not abrogated or contradicted by a clear statement in the Qur'an or Hadith.

7. *Status Quo* (*istiṣḥāb*)

If a dispute was brought to court, the status quo would be upheld until evidence appeared to the contrary. For example, if one party claimed property in the possession of a second party, the property remained with the second party until the first provided sufficient evidence to support the claim. Similarly, in any kind of dispute, the status quo is generally upheld by the law until evidence is produced to the court to change it: for example, a person is deemed mentally competent unless the court can be satisfied that he is not; a child under seven remains in the care of the mother unless the court is provided with good reasons to remove the mother's right of care.

8. *Blocking avenues of temptation* (*sad al-dharā'i*ᶜ)

The *naṣṣ* make very clear what is forbidden to believers. However, there are circumstances in which something not in itself forbidden leads so inevitably and predictably to that which is explicitly forbidden, that it too must be proscribed. The proscription is, naturally, expressed as narrowly as possible so as to avoid enlarging the domain of the forbidden. For example, a nightclub would not be allowed to operate if its operation was known to be encouraging Muslims to meet to drink alcohol or engage in some other forbidden activity such as gambling or prostitution. The danger of something leading to the forbidden does not by itself justify prohibiting it: the danger must be general and of a high degree. At the same time, the harm done by prohibiting something must be weighed against the good done by not doing so. If the possibility of harm is seen as slight compared to the benefit, the danger must simply be accepted and any wrongdoing corrected as it arises. Thus, it is permissible to cultivate grapes (which have many wholesome uses) in spite of the possibility that they can be made into wine; the making and selling of wine are nonetheless forbidden.

When the possibility of an action leading to a bad outcome is high, restriction is more likely. But in some situations, the decision on what is likely to be or become more harmful or more beneficial is difficult to make. It is mostly in situations of this kind that the Islamic jurists have disagreed with one another. For example, under Islamic law, once a husband (who is mentally competent to do so) has pronounced divorce for a third time, the divorce is final and the man, however much he may regret his action, cannot call his ex-wife back into the marriage unless she marries another man and is divorced by him. Now if both parties, ex-husband and ex-wife, regret the divorce, it is a hurt for them, which hurt the law will not permit the parties to undo unless the woman re-marries and is divorced. In such a situation, Imām Shāfiʿī and Imām Abū Ḥanīfah allowed a marriage to be arranged by the ex-husband for his ex-wife so that she might then be re-divorced, enabling him to re-marry her and the formerly divorced couple to re-unite. However, any such arrangement was proscribed by Imām Mālik and Imām Aḥmad ibn Ḥanbal: perhaps they felt that the Islamic law is as it is in order to make people realize that divorce is a very grave matter, and allowing a divorce to be undone even by wholly consensual arrangements would be to diminish its gravity in law.

BALANCING BENEFIT AND HARM

As the last example has illustrated, it is never a straightforward task to determine, in any particular situation, the ruling that will best promote good or best prevent harm. However, the importance and generality of the principle cannot be over-stated. The Shariʿah is intended to serve the best interest of mankind as a whole and for all time, not the interest of a particular racial or social group, or the tastes or moods of a particular epoch. The concept of 'best interest' encompasses the spiritual and mental well-being of all people in the present and the future. We have a strong and famous example in the decision of the second caliph, ʿUmar ibn al-Khaṭṭāb, to forbid the distribution of conquered territories in Iraq and Persia among the conquering troops, on the ground that if he did so, future generations would be deprived of land and the wealth it might generate.

As well as seeking the best interests of mankind as a whole, Islamic legislation is directed towards avoidance of harm. One of the cardinal maxims among Islamic jurists is derived from the Prophet's saying, "No hurt, no damage in Islam."[4] Any harmful procedure or transaction, any individual or collective behavior, that can cause hurt or damage can be prohibited in Islamic law. There should be: (1) no harm to oneself; (2) no harm to fellow human beings; and (3) no harm to the interests of society in general. The application of this maxim in situations where an individual may do hurt to himself or to persons in his care or to property which he controls (in which, through inheritance, others have a direct interest), whether wilfully or through incompetence, is of particular relevance to the subject-matter of this study.

When the interests of one party are associated with harm to another, the Shariʿah seeks ways by which to achieve a compromise. One of the ways to effect a compromise is the acceptance of minor harm to achieve a major interest. For example, preservation of a person's life is more important than preservation of his wealth. If a situation arises where, in order to preserve life or health, wealth must be dispensed to a degree that for any other purpose might be construed as squandering or waste, then such expenditure would be deemed justifiable in law. In some situations a harm has to be tolerated by the court in order to achieve a good purpose. For example, it is always undesirable to withdraw from any person his rights under the law, but in the case of a father known to pose a danger to the well-being of his children, the undesirable would have to be accepted and the father's right of custody would be removed in favour of another relative more likely to promote the welfare of the children. Analogously, the interests and rights of a group or of society as a whole would, in the event of conflict between the two, be preferred to the interests and rights of an individual.

In sum, we may affirm the remarkable power of the Shariʿah to adjust to different situations in order to serve its overall purpose of promoting the good and preventing the harmful. Between good and bad, the preference must be for good; between two harms or dangers, the lesser must be chosen; for the sake of the greater good, a minor harm can be tolerated; where the harm or benefit from a course of action are expected to be the same, or if the outcome cannot be calculated, then it is the harm that must be prevented.

This power of adjustment in the law is not something contrived by the scholars; its authority derives, as we noted earlier, from the explicit exemptions in the primary sources of the law (the *naṣṣ*) to the prescriptions that are found in the same sources. Therefore, in making these adjustments the great scholars of Islamic law were not seeking to subvert the law by clever devices, but rather to work, through the most meticulous attention to its letter, in harmony with its spirit and purpose.

JUDICIAL SYSTEM IN ISLAMIC LAW[5]

Under Islamic law, the caliph is the primary guardian of the religious and political life of the society, responsible for the proper functioning of the law, and he may, if he chooses, take on judicial duties himself or delegate a portion of them to others. The Prophet himself both acted as judge and appointed others as judges. The *khulafāʾ al-rāshidūn* (the rightly-guided caliphs) followed this example. In particular, they supervised or took personal charge of administrative judicial duties within the *diwān al-maẓālim* (literally, 'office of complaints'). Civil and criminal jurisdiction were left to appointed judges who would, on occasion, also run the administrative courts.

Courts of Ordinary Jurisdiction

The 'ordinary courts' handle the daily business of the law, essentially any matters that the head of state decides not to have under his own control. Judges have authority to deliver their own judgments on matters not legislated by the Qur'an and Sunnah. As well as deciding on civil and commercial matters, family and personal law, the judges tried criminal cases and decreed the Shariʿah punishments (*ḥudūd*) and sometimes the discretionary punishments (*taʿzīr*). The judges also supervised such matters as marrying girls who have no legal guardian, executing wills to safeguard the interests of orphans, and appointing guardians to their estates. Such functions had been carried out by the Prophet himself for a time. In the earliest period of Islamic history, judges appointed by the head of state sometimes also held responsibilities for political and administrative affairs. Later, as the Islamic state system evolved, politics and administration were separated from judicial affairs and a specialized body of judges was established.

The Administrative Judicial System

The 'office of complaints' was so called because it looked into complaints against government officials, high and low, and against judges, including the head of state. This office was set up to protect people from abuses of power. The person in charge of it had to be an authoritative judge of the highest calibre, with personal charisma, who commanded respect and obedience and who was known for fairmindedness, humility, piety and incorruptibility. He was charged not only to follow up complaints when presented, but also to look into matters on his own initiative if he had reason to suspect wrongdoing.

The 'office of complaints' had a remit that make its functioning very similar to what is practiced as administrative law in contemporary systems in different parts of the world. The administrative court under Islamic law in practice enjoyed a higher authority than the 'ordinary courts'. It had powers to conduct investigations and to use any appropriate strategies to obtain information about wrongdoing. It had responsibility to reach decisions and to issue verdicts on the matters (or persons) investigated and, where appropriate, to call witnesses, and to offer compromises that would resolve disputes between the contending parties. The complaints dealt with did not only come from the general public, the grievances of officials against their superiors were also judged within the *diwān al-maẓālim*. This kind of administrative court was not an Islamic innovation. It was prac-ticed by the kings of Persia, and also practiced in Arabia before Islam through what were known as 'treaties' between rival tribes. The Prophet investigated complaints against officials himself, and his caliphs did so likewise. The Umayyad caliph ʿUmar ibn ʿAbd al-ʿAzīz was the first to set aside a particular day of the week for dealing with such matters.

THE SYSTEM OF COURTS

The Concept of a 'Court'

Most of the classical works deal with the conditions under which the judge can function, detailing his responsibilities and the limits of his authority. They do not dwell upon the concept of a 'court' as such, nor use a term for it. They do, however, speak of a 'place of judgment', meaning by it the specialization in a particular area of the law, geographical locale to which the authority of the judge was limited, and the place where (and where only) cases could be heard. It is clearly stated in the works of the early scholars that an official judgment could only be handed out in the place designated for hearings. Also, judges with jurisdiction in a particular location could not hear cases in any other. Judges whose jurisdiction was restricted to certain areas of the law were given special titles to reflect the specialization. Besides such specializations as family law, commercial law, or criminal law, a judge could be specialized for a certain class of people or function, for example, the army, the police, or farmers, and so on. If there were two or more judges in one area, each with his own specialty, it was acceptable to have more than one judge in one geographic location. A judge who had authority to look into all matters of the law was called the 'judge of general inspection'.

Court Levels

Just as Islamic law recognized that courts and jurisdictions could be specialized, it also recognized that the courts could be classified into different levels. This has been established practice since at least the reign of the second caliph, ʿUmar ibn al-Khaṭṭāb. At that time, a judge was appointed to look into simpler cases, with more senior judges, and the caliph himself, looking into more serious matters. Similarly, there were judges who specialized in deciding financial disputes not exceeding a certain amount of money and others whose jurisdiction covered the higher amounts.

The concept of referral or appeal from a lower to a higher court had been known before then, since the time of the Prophet himself. In a case that became a famous precedent, ʿAlī ibn Abī Ṭālib, the Prophet's cousin, made this statement: "Since the Prophet is not here at this time, my decision will stand. However, if he comes back, and either the plaintiff or the defendant is unwilling to accept the decision, they can appeal to the Prophet himself." ʿAlī's decision was in fact appealed, and the Prophet upheld it. Subsequently, as well as recognizing that the decision of a court can be referred to a higher authority (usually the governor), Islamic law also recognized the concept of appealing the appeal itself, that is, of reviewing the whole trial process.

Judicial Proceedings in Contemporary Islamic Courts

Courts proceedings in many Islamic countries now follow a secular system usually derived, with some modifications, mainly form the French legal system. Family law is probably the only exception, since all Islamic countries follow the Shariʿah in matters related to marriage, divorce and child custody. A very few Islamic countries do not have a codified written law and use strictly Islamic jurisprudence as their only system in both civil and criminal proceedings. Increasingly, however, Islamic countries are now trying to use traditional Islamic law as the main or, whenever possible, the only, source of law practiced in their courts. They usually have to review past legal precedents, beginning in the earliest period in the time of Prophet Muhammad, and ending in the time of the Ottoman empire in the nineteenth century.

Islamic Countries Today

Saudi Arabia, since its birth some 70 years ago, is the prime example of an Islamic country that has not been influenced by any Western type of legal system. In this section, by way of illustrating contemporary Islamic practice, we will review briefly the organization of judicial proceedings in Saudi Arabia.

Courts in Saudi Arabia are headed by judges, typically by a single judge and rarely by a panel of judges. Courts of general jurisdiction see all cases, criminal and civil, including cases related to family matters. Criminal matters are now usually referred by an equivalent of a District Attorney who makes preliminary inquiries about the case from the police and the accused, and who decides whether or not the case will go to court. The post of 'District Attorney' has only been implemented in Saudi Arabia since the last decade. I participated in the first course given to train Law School graduates as 'District Attorneys.' Before that, criminal cases had been referred by the police directly. Civil cases can be initiated by the people involved directly, and/or through their lawyers.

In Egypt, Iraq, Syria, and most other Islamic countries, the courts run on two levels, a court of common pleas, and a higher court of appeals. The latter reviews all cases that are appealed for any reason, whether a matter of law or a matter of fact is the cause of review. Also, it may, unlike the courts of appeal in the American or British systems, retry the whole case rather than look at matters of law only. A third level of court, somewhat equivalent to the appeal court in the Anglo-American system, looks at cases which are appealed after the review from the second level court, and it restricts the review to matters of law only, excluding matters of fact.

According to Dr. Muḥammad M. Hāshim's book, '*Al-Qaḍā' wa Niẓām al-Ithbāt*,[6] there do not exist two levels of courts at present in Saudi Arabia. That is to say, all courts are considered as on the same level. There are, however, courts for 'Urgent Cases', the 'General Courts' are also called 'Superior Court' and 'Court of Appeals.' The last functions as the only avenue for review and only looks at an earlier court decision for fouls or mistakes in matters of law, it does not review the facts in the case. In other words, the appeal court will only criticize an earlier decision if there had been a violation of a rule in the Qur'an or Sunnah. In the event of a violation of Shariʿah, the case is remanded for retrial to the same court that made the earlier decision. Not all cases can be appealed. Minor cases where a fine to five hundred riyals (approximately 133 US dollars) or less is at issue cannot be appealed, nor if the decision had been reviewed already by a chief justice, nor if the case was not appealed within fifteen days from the announcement of the decision.

Cases referred to the Court of Appeals in Saudi Arabia are decided by a panel of three judges. However, decisions involving execution, amputation of a body part or death by stoning are decided by a panel of five judges.

The Saudi Arabian system does allow for review of matters of fact and retrials in certain cases. For example, where a court decision was made in the absence of the accused who then turned up. A retrial can also be announced if substantial new facts have appeared that require a revision of an earlier court decision.

It is important to note that cases related to administrative laws, like the Labor Law, do not come under the jurisdiction of the court system in Saudi Arabia. There are special committees set up to look into administrative matters, and these follow a different system.

A psychiatrist, or any expert witness for that matter, can be called to testify by the judge. The judge might initiate this testimony on his own or upon the request of the litigating parties, if he agrees to the request. Lawyers are not routinely involved in all cases, but their participation is acceptable if the parties involved wish it. In legal practice to date, it is quite rare for a psychiatrist to be asked to testify in person. Judges are usually content to receive a medical report and base their decision on that. In my experience, judges in Saudi Arabia have rarely made a decision that disagreed with an expert medical or psychiatric recommendation.

CHAPTER ONE

Privileges and Confidentiality

THE DOCTOR-PATIENT RELATIONSHIP

The psychiatrist as a physician owes to the patient the duty of care, through the establishment of doctor–patient relationship in a professional manner. In any legal conflict between doctor and patient, duty of care is a primary issue. Psychiatrists in general, and for that matter physicians in general, have no legal obligation to provide emergency medical care not specified in a statutory or contractual obligation. Having no legal obligation does not mean having no moral obligation. An off-duty physician who acts in an emergency is doing so out of a moral obligation and not a legal one under the secular laws.[1] Psychiatrists in private practice may choose whomever they wish to treat. However, once a psychiatrist has agreed explicitly or implicitly to accept a patient, he is under ethical and legal obligation to provide continuous care until the relationship is appropriately terminated.

The expressed or implied agreement by a psychiatrist to treat a patient in exchange for a fee serves to create a recognizable relationship with corresponding duties and rights for both parties. The legal foundation for the doctor–patient relationship is contract law. However, the duty of care is not predicated on the payment of fee but instead on the manifest agreement by the physician to render service. In other words, the agreement or contract created is based upon what is called a 'fiduciary'. Initiating the professional relationship does not constitute any guarantee for a specific result, but it does promise that the psychiatrist will exercise reasonable care. The doctor–patient relationship is not created in a situation where the psychiatrist is performing an evaluation only, that is, giving a diagnosis without also undertaking treatment. When a third party, such as a court or an insurance company or an employer, is the primary beneficiary of a psychiatric examination, that does not constitute a doctor–patient relationship.[2] However, any minor benefit, such as a hint of advice or treatment, given along with an evaluation may suffice to establish a doctor–patient relationship.

Under the doctrine of respondent superior, a supervising or employing psychiatrist is considered, from the legal point of view, to be the master of those under his care and is liable for their acts. Psychiatrists who employ or supervise others may be held liable for the negligence or errors of the latter, even if they have had no direct contact with the patient.[3]

Fiduciary Role Avoiding Double Agency

The psychiatrist is under an obligation to act with good faith and strict confidence in dealing with the patient. This obligation is inherent in all psychiatrist–patient relationships as an ethical and fiduciary duty. A professional in a fiduciary capacity is not allowed to use the relationship with the patient for personal benefit. A double agent role may arise if the psychiatrist simultaneously serves an agency and treats a patient in that agency. When this conflict arises, the patient should be made aware of the situation so that his consent to it is an informed consent.

A psychiatrist is legally required to provide treatment until the relationship is appropriately terminated, otherwise he can be sued for abandonment should the patient suffer any harm thereafter. Appropriate termination might involve either a unilateral act or the patient's withdrawal from treatment. A mutual agreement when services are no longer needed or useful, or a unilateral act on the part of the psychiatrist, terminates a treatment with appropriate referral for continuation of the patient's management. The psychiatrist is required, upon the request of the patient, to find another therapist and provide a record of information for the new therapist to follow.[4]

Confidentiality

It is the right of the patient to have his written and spoken communications held in confidence and not disclosed to outside parties without his prior authorization. The law has acknowledged this right of protection by including provisions for confidentiality in professional licensing laws and in privilege statutes. This protection is also contained in the ethical codes of various mental health professions. The developing case law has extended the same protetion as attorney–client privilege to include physicians and psychotherapists. Finally, the right of confidentiality may be subsumed under the constitutional right of privacy.

Once the doctor–patient relationship has been created, the professional automatically assumes a duty to safeguard a patient's disclosures. However, this duty is not absolute. There are certain circumstances in which breach of confidentiality is both ethical and legal. Naturally, the most common circumstance in which this confidentiality is broken is when the patient himself waives this right, as is his privilege (known as the 'testimonial privilege'), in favor of a specific authority or party. If the patient waives testimonial privilege, medical records may be sent to potential employers or insurance companies. At times the patient has the privilege of only partial waiver of confidentiality, as when he has participated in group therapy, for example. Many statutes mandate disclosure by psychiatrists in one or more situations.[5]

Privilege

Privilege statutes represent the most common recognition by the state of the importance of protecting information provided by a patient to a psychiatrist. Privilege as a concept refers to the patient's right to hold in private or release any information that has been communicated to his physician. In other words, the patient and not the psychiatrist is the holder of the privilege that governs the withholding or release of confidential information. The privilege of the patient to keep his record in confidence is protected from disclosure even in court. However, this protection is fairly limited and there are many circumstances in which the privilege may be lost. The protection provided by the privilege is justified on the basis that the special need for privacy in the doctor–patient relationship outweighs the need for full and accurate disclosure of information in court, except in very particular circumstances. In the U.S. the exceptions vary from one state to another; however, the most common are:

1. reports of child abuse;
2. involuntary hospitalization;
3. court order evaluation;
4. cases in which a patient's mental status is in question during litigation relating to a contested will, worker compensation, child custody disputes, personal injuries, and malpractice suits;
5. protection of a third party.

The last exception, still somewhat controversial, refers to the duty of the psychiatrist to protect the public by warning threatened individuals. It followed the famous Tarasoff case in 1974 when the California Supreme Court ruled that doctors or therapists bear duty to use reasonable care to get threatened persons such warning as is essential to avert foreseeable danger arising from a patient's condition. One of the famous alliterative quotes from this case is, "Protective privilege ends when the public peril begins."[6] This ruling was revised and clarified in 1976:

> When a therapist determines or pursuant to the standards of his profession should determine that his patient presents a serious danger of violence to another, he incurs an obligation to use reasonable care to protect the intended victim against such danger. The discharge of this duty may require the therapist to take one or more various steps depending upon the nature of the case. Thus, it may call for him to warn the intended victim or others likely to apprise the victim of the danger, notify police, or take whatever steps that are reasonably necessary under the circumstances.[7]

Despite this clarification, controversy persisted and there have been further attempts to revise the ruling.

DOCTOR-PATIENT RELATIONSHIP IN ISLAMIC LAW

In Islamic law the nature of the doctor–patient relationship is contractual. However, under Islamic law, unlike secular law, there is no formal distinction between the legal and the moral duties. The contract has a professional part and a moral part and the doctor must adhere to all the conditions of the contract. He must abide by the principles of the medical profession and is liable for mistakes or neglect. He is also held responsible for any violation of the principles committed by his assistants or any others involved in the patient's care.[8]

As required by the ethics of the medical profession, the doctor should be gentle, pleasant and well-mannered, try to make things easy for the patient, and stress the optimistic aspects of his condition. He must avoid unpleasant statements and unpleasant expressions and must not exaggerate the seriousness of the condition.[9]

The doctor cannot refuse treatment to a patient if there is no other doctor available. This principle has been derived from traditions of the Prophet: it is unlawful for a group of people to let any member of the group go hungry;[10] a person who has enough water and yet refuses to provide it to one who is thirsty will be punished;[11] if a person finds an animal belonging to someone he knows caught in a trap and does not release the animal, he is liable for its loss and obliged to give compensation to the owner.[12]

As Islamic law has been so careful to prevent human suffering as to make it obligatory for a human to save his fellow-human from such misfortunes as thirst, hunger, or loss of property, the treatment of a sick person can by analogy be presumed to be a more serious obligation. Accordingly, Islamic law has made it obligatory for the physician to treat a patient irrespective of any compensation he may receive. However, the fact that the physician is obliged to treat patients does not deny him the right of compensation. The right to a fee was stressed by Abū Ḥanīfah[13] as well as by some of the Ḥanbalī scholars.[14] However, other branches of the Ḥanbalī school and the Shāfiʿīs were of the opinion that the physician is obliged to treat the sick without compensation, although the patient may volunteer a fee if he is so inclined.[15]

Guarantee of Outcome

Guarantee of outcome, i.e. a cure, is not required, as long as the physician meets the minimal requirement of being 'qualified'. Islamic jurisprudence describes 'a qualified physician' as being a 'skillful' physician, and 'skillful' means an individual known to make mistakes only rarely. A person who, in a particular place and time, is not recognized as 'qualified' to practice as a physician will be liable for any mistake; in order to escape punishment or being prosecuted for damages he will be expected to guarantee a safe outcome or cure.[16]

Abandonment of a Patient

In Islamic law, abandonment of the patient is equivalent to refusal of treatment. There is no disagreement among Islamic scholars that a physician who abandons his patient is committing a sin punishable by God. However, the physician's liability for abandonment and its consequences vary according to different scholars. The Ḥanafīs and the Mālikīs hold that a specific punishment should be decreed by a judge while the Ḥanbalīs and the Shāfiʿīs hold that the sin is indeed punishable by God but that there is no specific punishment to be inflicted on the physician.[17] However, there is a general principle that obedience to the laws of the land is mandatory, so long as these rules do not violate the basic Islamic principles. Therefore, if the government or the legislative body in an Islamic state passes a law making abandonment illegal, then the doctor must abide by that law and violation is punishable under the law.[18]

DIAGNOSES AND PSYCHIATRIC EVALUATION

Under secular law, a psychiatric evaluation alone, as ordered by a judge or other authorities competent to do so, without consequent treatment, is considered a 'practice of medicine'. By contrast, the Arabic definition means by 'practice of medicine' the actual process of treatment. If no treatment is rendered, the doctor–patient relationship is not established through evaluation alone.[19]

Psychiatrist as Expert Witness

According to the so-called 'opinion exclusion rule', it is the responsibility of the judge or jury to determine the facts of a case, to form an opinion thereon, and eventually reach a verdict. The function of a witness is therefore restricted to statement of facts, not opinions about the facts. On the other hand, if scientific, technical, or other specialized knowledge will help the judge to understand the evidence or to determine a fact, a witness qualified as an expert by knowledge, skill, experience, training or education may give an opinion testimony in his area of expertise. When psychiatrists testify they usually do so as experts, although they might also be summoned as fact witnesses.[20]

Expert testimony is well known and extensively studied in the literature of Islamic law. It is generally acknowledged that in certain circumstances, professionals are needed to provide specific or general opinion. Their testimony is held in good esteem in the Islamic court. The expert witness should be recognized as an expert and a professional within the specialty in which he is testifying.[21]

Islamic law makes a distinction between expert testimony (a) as relevant to a particular case for a particular defendant, and (b) as a general statement, not necessarily linked to a particular case. For example, a psychiatrist might be asked to define and explain the nature of schizophrenic illness with or without reference to a particular case. This distinction is quite similar to what is distinguished under secular law as an 'opinion' or 'fact' testimony. Each kind of expert testimony, whether it be specific or non-specific, has its own conditions and requirements.

If the psychiatrist or the expert is testifying on general principles without reference to a particular case, then, contrary to the well-known rule that a minimum of two witnesses is mandatory, a testimony from a single person recognized in his field as an expert, is accepted. Also, in this kind of testimony, the testimony of one woman is accepted if her specialty is relevant to women's matters, such as gynaecology.[22]

Expert testimony, if referring to a particular case, must be substantiated by at least two expert witnesses. It is assumed that since this testimony refers to a particular case, it carries the same weight as witnessing a particular event and testifying to that. In this case, the testimony of a woman might not be accepted unless it is corroborated by three other women. Women's expert testimony is called for only if needed, and when the issue in question is considered a woman's matter, such as gynaecological problems or psychosexual disorders.

If the testimony is of a general nature and not specific to a particular case, it could be viewed as a statement of opinion. Some jurists have not considered this a witness testimony, but rather a matter from which the court will gain information and as a source of knowledge.[23]

The expert witness status enjoys another exemption from the general rule. In Islamic law, the testimony of a non-Muslim is not accepted against a Muslim defendant. However, scholars have accepted expert testimony from a non-Muslim physician under certain conditions, namely that he is recognized as an expert by the court; that his testimony is general and does not refer to the particulars of the case in question; and that there is no available Muslim expert to testify to the same matter.[24]

PRIVILEGES AND CONFIDENTIALITY IN ISLAMIC LAW

Under secular rules, there are different moral codes for different professions. It might happen in certain circumstances that the practice of the medical profession demands an action that is contradictory to the practice of the legal profession. In such a case, a conflict might arise. However, under Islamic law, the moral code of the religion is the main source of legislative morality in all professions, including the medical and legal. It is assumed that no discrepancy or conflict will arise between the moral codes of medical practice and religious or state legislated morality.

Confidentiality in Islam is highly esteemed. Keeping private matters confidential within the professional system is strongly emphasized in the Qur'an and Hadith. In a number of traditions of the Prophet, there is a statement to the effect that betrayal of a confidence is a major sin. The Qur'an refers to and stresses the value of 'keeping a promise'.[25] Maintaining the confidentiality between physician and patient falls within the general command to keep one's promises. The Prophet made a statement to the effect that God will protect whoever keeps the secret of a Muslim from being disclosed.[26] He also said that hypocrites have three characteristics, one of which is betrayal of confidences.[27] He also made a statement to the effect that if a person was told something in confidence, the confidence would be of the nature of an *amānah* (literally, 'trust'). Since the term *amānah* can cover the holding of confidences, and since carrying and delivering a trust with integrity is a highly charged religious obligation in Islam, the importance of maintaining confidentiality is self-evident. Its importance is fully reflected in the pertinent rules of law.[28]

There are a number of general rules in Islamic legal practice relating to patient confidentiality. These include:

1. A doctor may not be required to testify against his patient. If he volunteers such testimony, it will not usually be accepted. Generally in Islamic jurisprudence, testimony is not accepted from a witness who is too eager to give it. Testimony is only accepted if it is requested by the plaintiff or defendant.

2. If a physician testifies that his patient has committed a sin that requires a certain punishment, his testimony will not be accepted as a confession from the patient. This is so whether the doctor was forced or volunteered to give the information. A confession is only accepted if the person responsible for the act himself confesses to it before the judge.

3. In no circumstances can the physician be forced by law to disclose confidential matters concerning a patient. Ibn Ḥajar has stressed the importance of keeping confidences secret in the face of pressure from the judge or a ruler.[29] He puts the responsibility for any disclosure on the doctor's judgment. If the doctor feels that to disclose a patient's secret may have more serious consequences than not to disclose it; or if disclosure may result in some harm to the patient or to others in excess of the benefit that would come out of disclosure, he has the right to keep the matter confidential and not reveal it, even to a judge. In fact, Ibn Ḥajar also stressed that if a ruler puts pressure on a physician to reveal a secret with threats, the physician is permitted to lie and his doing so will not be considered a sin.[30]

In principle, Islamic law does recognize exception to the law of confidentiality. However, it does not specify the particular circumstances (such as child abuse or involuntary hospitalization, etc.) which would justify the exception. Because Islamic law does not empower the judge to force a physician to reveal the patient's secret, the primary responsibility for disclosure or non-disclosure rests with the physician himself. The relevant general principles are that one wrong or harm should not be avoided by another wrong or harm, and that, in the face of having to choose between two evils, the 'lesser evil' must be chosen. With these principles in mind, the physician must decide whether breaching the confidence will be more beneficial to the patient or the community in general or to other particular people involved. Child abuse cases would be considered an exception to the confidentiality rule if the physician considers that a greater good will be served by disclosure. If the physician feels that a patient's involuntary hospitalization will bring more benefit to that patient and/or to the society, then he might disclose some confidential matters in order to keep the patient in the hospital. The same will apply in the case of protecting others from danger or harm, as in the example of the Tarasoff case mentioned above. In general, under Islamic law, the physician is under no obligation to make exceptions to the confidentiality law through the orders of court or any kind of external pressure. However, making such exceptions is permissible as explained and in the situation where the patient himself sees that more benefit can come from the exception than harm.

The general rule is to respect privacy; even when the patient discloses the worst sin his privacy has to be respected even in the face of a judge's order. On the other hand, if an individual's behavior is thought likely to entice others or affect them negatively, then a physician may be allowed to reveal that individual's secret. Imām Ḥanbal made a statement to the effect that a person's secret should be kept unless it is a threat to, or a bad influence on, others. Al-Nawawī supported the view that a man's secret should be disclosed if it becomes a threat to other people's interests. It is important to emphasize that any decision about disclosure is still left to the physician's judgment, that the judge may not expect or force him to make disclosure.[31]

The physician who purposely reveals confidential material about his patient is, first, liable for damage incurred and, second, subject to punishment. Since there is no specific punishment mentioned in the Qur'an and Sunnah, it is usually determined by the local judge. Such punishment falls under the rubric of *taʿzīr,* which is defined as any kind of punishment (in the form of jail sentence or otherwise) not specified in the Qur'an or in the Sunnah. *Taʿzīr* punishments were usually decreed by the ruler and passed in the form of a sentence by the judge.[32]

THE SUBPOENA IN SECULAR AND ISLAMIC LAW

Attorneys who are involved in active litigation have an absolute right to obtain a subpoena by merely attesting to a belief that certain individuals have information that is relevant to the lawsuit. A subpoena does not have the legal force of a court order. A court order commands someone to do or not to do something. The subpoena obliges the witness, who may be a psychiatrist, to appear in court in order to testify. However, it does not order him specifically to testify. In medical litigation, a subpoena can be of two kinds: a subpoena that includes medical records and a subpoena that requires oral testimony only. If the psychiatrist, or anybody for that matter, refuses to obey a subpoena to appear in court, he risks citation for contempt of court and the legal consequences, which could include a jail sentence. If compelled to testify, the psychiatrist is ethically obliged to provide only information that is relevant to the specific issue before the court. A request to testify about information that is irrelevant or that appears to exceed the scope of the court order should be questioned directly and appealed to the judge. If the psychiatrist feels that his client will be hurt by his testimony, or if there is no competent consent from the patient, the patient's attorney or the psychiatrist may file a motion to quash the subpoena on the basis of protection under physician–patient privilege and the duty to maintain confidentiality. The judge will decide on the motion to settle the question whether or not the psychiatrist must testify or turn over the records.

The Qur'anic verse "... and let no harm be done to scribe or witness" (2:282) was interpreted by some scholars to mean that no force should be put upon any person to testify or to appear in court. Therefore, the question of whether to testify and reveal the record and so breach confidentiality remains one for the physician to decide. In general, the physician or the psychiatrist has an absolute right to keep matters relevant to his patient in strict confidence. However, he is allowed to exercise conscience and judgment as to whether disclosure will help the patient or others, or will do more harm than good.

CHAPTER TWO

Insanity Defense and Criminal Responsibility

IN SECULAR LAW (THE ANGLO-AMERICAN TRADITION)

Components of Crime

A crime, in the formal legal sense of the word, has two components: an act that is forbidden by law (*actus reus*) and a guilty intent (*mens rea*). To be called a crime an act must be committed voluntarily and knowingly with a specific and purposeful intent. To establish specific intent beyond reasonable doubt is part of the task of the prosecuting advocate.

No Intent, No Crime, or a Lesser Offense

The earliest concept of criminal responsibility is attributed to Aristotle: "A person is morally responsible if, with knowledge of the circumstances, in the absence of external compulsion, he deliberately chooses to commit a specific act."[1] The key elements here are knowledge and choice.

At the beginning of the eleventh century, most forms of homicide and other injuries were treated as matters for compensation under threat of feud. The crime was held against reparation; in the case of the insane, the family was held responsible for compensation.[2] By the end of that century, certain crimes were no longer considered suitable for civil compensation. They were called 'bootless' and the state took over punishment of these crimes, which might include murder and some kinds of theft.

In the year 1268, Henry Bracton merged the strict liability of secular law and the moral intent of Church Law, thus initiating the intent component (*mens rea*) of crime which still exists in Anglo-American common law.[3]

Understanding Right and Wrong

The concept of 'non-criminal responsibility' for one who is unable to be aware, or has no understanding, of the nature of the act he has committed can be traced as far back as the eighteenth century BC Hammurabi Code in ancient Mesopotamia. Also, the Babylonian *Talmud* states: "a deaf-mute, imbecile or a minor – he who wounds them is culpable, but if they wound others, they are not culpable."[4]

In Roman law, if a child or an insane person committed homicide, he was not held accountable because "the one is excused by the innocence of his intentions, the other by the fact of his misfortune." Blackstone's commentaries in the eighteenth century suggested that children under seven year of age were not responsible for crime; children over fourteen years were responsible. That left children between seven and fourteen years liable to conviction if it could be established that they could at least distinguish between good and evil.[5]

THE INSANITY DEFENSE

The 'Wild Beast' Standard

It is important to note that the periodic or cyclic nature of some mental illnesses was not recognized until the thirteenth century. Prior to the 1500s, insane persons in England were convicted for their crimes but then granted a royal pardon upon request of the jury. The first clear-cut acquittal case due to insanity occurred in 1505. In 1724, in the famous trial of R. vs. Arnold, the justice charged the jury with the following accord, which became a landmark in insanity defense: "A man must be totally deprived of his understanding and memory so as not to know what he is doing, no more than an infant, a brute, or a wild beast."[6] This trial established the 'total insanity' or 'wild beast' standard in England for more than 75 years. It was not until the nineteenth century that courts took an interest in the content of the madman's delusion and the extent to which it motivated his deeds.

'Offspring of Delusion'

Another landmark case occurred in 1800. This concerned James Hadfield who, in a premeditated act, shot at King George III as he entered the royal box in a theater. He was charged and tried for treason. Hadfield did not meet the 'wild beast' or 'total insanity' test, although it was proven that he acted on strict delusion. The jury found Hadfield not guilty by reason of insanity and a new criterion for insanity was developed from delusion rather than a lack of all understanding, as in the 'wild beast' test. This criterion was called the 'offspring of delusion'.

'Irresistible Impulse'

In the Edward Oxford trial in 1840, the concept of insanity defense was established after Oxford committed the first of seven attempted assassinations of Queen Victoria. The jury was charged: "If some controlling disease was, in truth, the acting power within him which he could not resist, then he will not be responsible."[7] This constitutes the first judicial statement of the so-called 'irresistible impulse' test.

The McNaughton Case

The McNaughton trial in 1843 is probably the most famous of all criminal trials in the history of forensic psychiatry. It established a test and rule that became a standard for the insanity defense all over the world and remained so for more than a hundred years.

McNaughton, a Scottish wood-turner, felt persecuted for several years. He stalked the Prime Minister and tried to kill him but mistaking his identity killed the Prime Minister's secretary instead. At that time, four psychiatrists examined McNaughton and another two psychiatrists testified; a total of six psychiatrists agreed that McNaughton was insane and did not know the nature of his act. His attorney stressed that although the defendant was able to formulate a plan, it did not mean he acted as a responsible agent, because his 'moral faculties', not his intellect, were disordered.

McNaughton was acquitted by reason of insanity. This produced an intense outrage because the public felt that the criminal had been let off lightly. Fifteen judges of the Supreme Court of Judicatures were called together and asked McNaughton a number of questions. They expressed the concern of Queen Victoria. Following that, the McNaughton rule was established. The rule concludes:

> to establish a defense on the grounds of insanity, it must be clearly proven that at the time of committing the act, the party accused was laboring under such a defect of reason, from disease of the mind, as not to know the nature and quality of the act he was doing; or if he did know it, he did not know he was doing what was wrong and whether the accused, at the time of committing the act, knew the difference between right and wrong in respect to the very act with which he is charged.[8]

The McNaughton rule clearly recommended that the jury's question be shifted to whether the defendant knew that the specific criminal act was wrong.

The McNaughton rule established that the jury address the issue of moral vs. legal wrongfulness. "If the accused was aware that his act was one he ought not do, and if that act at the time was contrary to the law of the land, he is punishable."[9] In other words, it was his knowledge of his wrong-doing together with its illegality which made him punishable. The legal awareness of wrongfulness was not enough to make a person responsible for or aware of the criminality of his act. It should also be considered that awareness of moral wrong is relevant.

American jurisdiction, however, varies on moral or legal wrongfulness. In certain states, moral wrongfulness as a standard is accepted; however, in others, only awareness in the legal sense of wrongful is the standard. Judge Cardoza, a famous supreme court judge, interpreted McNaughton to mean that moral wrongfulness alone was sufficient. It follows that the knowledge of wrongfulness should have either one or two of the following standards:

1. The illegality standard: The accused lack criminal responsibility if, as a result of psychiatric disorder, they lack the capacity to know that their act violated the law.

2. The subjective moral standard: The accused lack criminal responsibility if, as a result of a psychiatric disorder, they believe that they were morally justified in their behavior, even though they may have known that their act was illegal and/or contrary to the public standard of morality.

3. The objective moral standard: The accused lack criminal responsibility if, as a result of a psychiatric disorder, they lack the capacity to know that society considered their act to be wrong, i.e., to know that their act was contrary to the public standards of morality.

It should be remembered that the presence of a mental illness is the most important component of these decisions. The fact that a man kills for moral reasons is not enough for him to be acquitted if he has no mental disorder.[10]

As noted above, the Edward Oxford trial in 1840 constituted the first reference by a judge to the concept of irresistible impulse. That rule has allowed English judges to give broad charges to juries to consider irresistible impulse in spite of the limitations of the McNaughton rule. In 1863, James Steven wrote that "total inability to refrain due to mental disease should qualify for insanity."[11] The irresistible impulse was clearly referred to in the Parson case in 1887, when it was asked: "If the defendant did not know the nature and quality of his act and that it was wrong, was he unable, because of mental disease or defect, to adhere to the right?"[12] However, by 1920 the irresistible impulse criterion was disqualified in England as an insanity defense. In the U.S. in 1957, following the Homicide Act, in certain states "substantially impaired responsibility" came to be interpreted on appeal as including the inability to exercise control over a physical act. From that point on, another arm was added to the insanity defense which is called "inability to refrain". In most of the United States it was included as part of the insanity defense and was incorporated in tests of insanity in some state laws.

More Recent Rulings on the Insanity Defense

The McNaughton test was used in the United States as the main criterion to decide on an insanity defense until 1954, when Judge Bazelone in Washington introduced a new test known as the 'Durham test'. It states that "the accused is not criminally responsible if his unlawful act is the product of mental disease or defect."[13]

This test is considered the most lenient and the most broadly interpreted, and has caused some problems, for instance, in the psychiatrist coming to usurp the jury's role, and in how to deal with psychopathic offenders, and an extremely high rate of acquittals by reason of insanity. The Durham rule has been abandoned throughout the United States and most of the rest of the world

It was replaced by another rule written by the American Law Institute in 1965 and incorporated in the Model Penal Code in 1965. It states (American Law Institute 1965):

1. "A person is not responsible for his criminal conduct if at the time of such conduct, as a result of mental disease or defect, he lacks substantial capacity to appreciate the criminality of his conduct or to conform his conduct to the requirement of the law."[14]

2. The terms 'mental disease' or 'defect' do not include an abnormality manifested only by repeated criminal or otherwise antisocial conduct.

This rule has in a sense softened the McNaughton concept from the criminal 'knowing' to 'appreciating' the criminality of his conduct, i.e., replacing the crucial term 'knowledge' with 'appreciation'. It also contains the 'irresistible impulse' or 'inability to refrain' concept insofar as "capacity to conform his conduct to the requirement of the law" is interpreted as the ability to refrain.[15]

This remained the primary rule controlling the insanity defense until 1988, when Ed Hinckly was tried for shooting President Reagan in 1984 and was acquitted as not guilty by reason of insanity. This caused Congress to pass a law governing the insanity defense in the United States, which was taken as a model for other countries as well. It states: "It is an affirmative defense to a prosecution under Federal statute that, at the time of the commission of the act constituting the offense, the defendant as a result of a severe mental disease or defect, was unable to appreciate the nature and quality of the wrongfulness of his act." In this rule, the word 'severe' was added and the cognitive aspects of the law were stressed by the use of the term 'appreciate' in "appreciate the nature and quality of the wrongfulness of his act."

However, there is no reference to the 'inability to refrain' concept in the American Psychiatric Association Statement on the Insanity Defense.[16]

IN ISLAMIC LAW

Criminal Intent

The concept of *mens rea*, guilty intent, is well accepted under Islamic law. There is no crime if there is no intention to commit it. Under Islamic law, the insane are recognized as lacking, or unable to have, an intention because of disturbed reasoning; therefore, they are not liable for the crimes they commit.

Crimes in general fall under two major categories as far as *mens rea* is concerned. Those with full intention are classed under *ʿamd* which means purpose, design, premeditation, and unintentional acts are classed under *khaṭāʾ*, which means error, mistake. Islamic law, however, recognizes a third kind of crime which is described as quasi-intentional, *shibh al-ʿamd*. This third category applies only in murder cases. For example, an angry person with the intention of assault and battery but without the intent to kill, may use a weapon that leads to death. This act would be classified as quasi-intentional.[17]

Murder with full intent is defined as an act that leads to death with the intention of causing it. Islamic law, however, does not recognize the difference between a crime that is premeditated and one that is not. Both of these crimes are punishable by death. It is important to note here that if the family of the victim decides to accept bloodwit (compensation) and not punish the murderer, the latter may be set free unless there is a decision by the governing authorities to give additional punishment. However, if the family of the victim decides not to accept the bloodwit, the governor does not have authority to modify the sentence.[18]

Quasi-Intentional Crime

The only crime that could be classified as quasi-intentional is murder. However, there is no consensus on this. Among the four major schools of Sunni law, three recognize this kind of crime. The school of Mālik does not recognize it and classifies murder in only two categories, those by intention and those by mistake. According to the Mālikī school, an assault that unintentionally leads to death is still treated as premeditated murder. The school of Shāfiʿī recognizes quasi-intentional crime in assault and battery, in addition to crimes of murder, that is to say quasi-intent is also accepted as a defense in cases of bodily harm that do not lead to death. A branch of the Ḥanbalī school and the Ḥanifi school do not recognize quasi-intent in assault and battery cases.[19]

It is important to note that, in Islamic law, the civil aspect of the crime is fully affirmed whether the crime was done with full intent or partial intent or by mistake: in all cases, civil liability holds, and compensation can be demanded.

THE CONCEPT OF INSANITY IN ISLAMIC LAW

The technical word for insanity in Arabic is *junūn*. The root meaning of the word from which *junūn* is derived is 'hidden' or 'invisible', indicating that insanity may have been considered a form of possession by invisible beings (*jinn* or demons). However, the technical meaning of *junūn* is insanity, the removal or spoiling of the mind or reason. Islamic scholars have defined insanity as "the impairment of the mind, where it prevents action and speech from operating on reason, except rarely."[20] In another definition, it is described as the "impairment of the power which distinguishes between fair and foul [good and evil] and conceives the consequences of those things. This power is no longer in evidence or it cannot do its function." Yet another definition is "the impairment of the power in which the conception of the whole is achieved."

Besides insanity, Islamic law recognizes two other mental conditions that are classified (by some scholars but not others) under the same rule as insanity in criminal responsibility. These are:

1. *Sudden perplexity*. The term used for this condition, *dahish*, translates as 'perplexed', 'startled', 'stunned'. It refers to the sudden loss of reason as a result of consternation, alarm or perplexity. In respect of criminal responsibility, the Ḥanafī school considers *dahish* along the same lines as insane.

2 *Mental retardation.* Islamic scholars recognized the difference between insanity as a disturbance of the mind and the condition that is currently termed 'mental retardation'. They gave it the name *ʿatah*. It is described as diminished ability of the mind to reason, and is distinguished from insanity or sudden perplexity. The term also covers dementia, and could be applied to cases of senile dementia as well as mental retardation. *ʿAtah* is ruled as insanity by the agreement of all scholars.

Islamic law also recognizes a particular mental condition called *safāhah*, which literally means extreme folly. It is not insanity, nor the consistent want of foresight that would indicate lower intelligence. A *safīh* person behaves in an irresponsible manner, for example squandering his money, and in certain conditions, may lose his civil rights. If a man or woman were seen to spend money recklessly, their family would have the right to file a complaint to classify them as *safīh* and they would then lose control over their money. According to some schools of Islamic law, the *safīh* may also forfeit other kinds of civil rights such as holding certain kinds of job or profession.[21]

CLASSIFICATION OF INSANITY IN ISLAMIC LAW

Islamic jurisprudence classifies insanity into three types: absolute (or continuous), intermittent, and partial.

Absolute (or Continuous) Insanity

In this condition the individual is judged to be completely and continuously unable to use his reason properly. It may begin at some point during the person's life or he may have been born with it. It can involve all aspects of perception, conception and reasoning including cognitive functions, or it can be less severe but lasting.

Intermittent Insanity

The state in which a person can sometimes communicate at a reasonable level of conception, perception and cognition, but at other times suffers complete loss of his mental faculties, moving between full or partial remission and normal function. Such a person will be considered insane and not culpable during the active state of his mental disorder. He will be fully responsible for all his actions when he is not in that state. When in partial remission, he will be culpable for things that he is able to conceive and appreciate.

Partial insanity

In this state the person will have the ability to appreciate the nature of some of his actions, and understand certain circumstances. However, in other areas of life and different circumstances, he lacks the same appreciation. He is able to conceive and recognize certain matters and is aware of the reality of his environment, but is unable to perform the same functions in relation to other matters. Periods of exacerbation and a state of absolute insanity can occur at certain times. The partially insane person is legally responsible for those actions he is able to conceive and perceive as they are in reality. At the same time, he is not culpable for other areas of his life which he is unable to appreciate.[22]

Mental Retardation and Dementia (*ʿAtah*)

ʿAtah is treated by the law in the same way as insanity when the condition is judged to be severe enough. It is judged to be severe enough when it impairs judgment to the extent that it causes inability to appreciate the nature of one's actions. However, mild degrees of retardation in an adult cause him to function at the level of a young boy. He might be able to differentiate some parts or aspects of his actions and behavior as being right or wrong. Islamic jurisprudence calls a youth who is so capable *al-ṣabī al-mummayiz* ('rational youth'). The term of course applies to females as well. The 'rational youth' has some responsibility and culpability insofar as he is con-sidered to have a degree of mental competence for particular actions. We believe that, by analogy, the legal reasoning applied to the 'rational youth' could be applied to patients who are diagnosed as retarded or demented but not severely enough to cause significant mental and cognitive impairment. This is a line of argument for contemporary Islamic scholars to pursue.

Sleep Disorders

In Islamic law, there is a special recognition of the state of sleep. Any movement during a state of sleep that results in an offense is treated under the same rule as insanity. The individual who walks in his sleep and commits a violation is not culpable. States analogous to sleep, or sleep disorders, might be included under this condition providing they are documented by the expert as such. These may include 'night terror', 'fugue states' and other kinds of 'hypnotic trance'.

Deaf-Mutes

Some schools of Islamic jurisprudence, such as that of Abū Ḥanīfah, believe that a deaf-mute, because of his disability and incapability of defending himself adequately, especially if he cannot write, would be difficult to prosecute. This difficulty might constitute what was termed *shubhah* or 'doubt'. If there is doubt about their ability to defend themselves, they are not able to participate in an adequate or fair trial and therefore cannot have the same status as a normal person. However, other schools such as the Mālikī, Shāfiʿī, and Ḥanbalī, believe that if a deaf-mute were able to admit to his crime by signaling, this admission could be taken into consideration.[23]

THE INSANITY DEFENSE IN THE TWO TRADITIONS

There is no disagreement about insanity and criminal responsibility in Islamic law, namely that an insane person is not culpable for any action he might commit. However, as we have seen, there are various definitions and conceptions of insanity:

Such impairment of the mind as prevents action and speech "operating on reason"; or "impairment of the power which distinguishes between fair and foul [good and evil]" and conceives the consequences thereof; and "impairment of the power in which the conception of the whole is achieved." The phrase "conception of the whole" in particular reflects a profound understanding of the nature of mental illness. It indicates that the mentally ill person might not be able to differentiate the whole from its parts. This reflects an understanding that mental health might be intact in certain areas but impaired in others, and that a disturbance of the faculty that integrates the parts in different aspects of life to make it whole is the essence of mental illness. We may note also that distinguishing "fair and foul [good and evil]"is equivalent to knowing right and wrong as it was clarified in the McNaughton ruling. Further, Islamic jurisprudence recognized diminished mental capacity in the absence of psychosis in such conditions as mental retardation and dementia and classified them into different levels.

Islamic law rules that there is "no duty or punishment for the insane," and "the pen is withheld from the insane person until he recovers." These two rules could permit the same latitude of interpretation as the Durham rule, since they do not place any restriction on the abnormality of mind that is insanity. The reform of the Durham rule by the Model Penal Code distinguished two arms of the insanity defense, that of 'knowing' and 'appreciating' the criminality of the action committed, or the cognitive from the affective aspect of being able to "conform [one's] conduct to the requirement of the law." The public outrage in response to the Hinckly acquittal led the U.S. Congress to pass a new rule which stresses the cognitive aspect of the insanity rule and puts little or no emphasis on the affective aspect, and ignores other arms of the insanity defense that deal with the so-called 'irresistible impulse' or 'ability to refrain'.

However, "to conform [one's] conduct to the requirement of the law" does imply the ability to refrain from persisting in conduct that does not conform. That ability, distinct from knowing or appreciating the criminality of a particular act, derives mainly from affective aspects of human behavior aptly summarized as 'ability to refrain'. As we saw, this was identified and discussed by Islamic scholars under the rubric of 'sudden perplexity' or *dahish*.

Some Islamic scholars included this condition under the same rule as insanity.[24] We believe that it is equivalent to 'temporary insanity' in modern forensic usage. Therefore, Islamic jurisprudence, at least in some schools, has acknowledged that, as a perplexed or startled person is temporarily in the same state as the insane, he should not be considered culpable under the law, and therefore to be ruled innocent by reason of insanity. Some scholars considered *dahish* to be a condition in which mind and reason are temporarily beyond voluntary control. Thus *dahish* could be referred to the states of mind termed under current secular law as 'irresistible impulse' and 'temporary insanity', both conditions that lead to impairment of the 'ability to refrain'. Islamic scholars have gone a step further by including severe obsession under the rule of insanity. This adds another aspect to Islamic law that is addressed in the secular law under the rubric of 'irresistible impulse'.[25]

Finally, we may note that Islamic law affirms the analogy of extreme rage with the state of insanity by declaring that a man who divorces his wife while enraged to the extent that he is not aware of his immediate reality, comes under the same rule as the insane and his declaration of divorce is not valid.[26]

CONCLUSION

It was not until the 1500s that the first confirmed insanity acquittal was recorded in Western history and the modern laws that govern insanity have been formulated over the last 500 years or less. It is rather impressive that Islamic law addressed this issue so sensitively and thoroughly in the seventh and eighth centuries. It seems that most of the arguments evolved in secular law were identified by Islamic scholars in the past and are accepted as reliable guidelines for Islamic legal judgements.

It is important to note that the presence of mental illness is never automatically equated with non-culpability. It was clearly stated that partial or intermittent insanity carries with it a level of responsibility, according to when and how far understanding of reality is impaired. If the nature of the crime is totally unrelated to the specific aspect of reality affected by the mental illness, the accused will be held fully responsible for his crime.

This view is affirmed in the fact that most scholars concluded that partially insane individuals were responsible for their actions if they recognized those particular actions as being right or wrong. It would be irrelevant here to differentiate between the legal recognition and the moral one since, within the context of Islamic jurisdiction, all matters of morality are derived from the doctrines of religion.

CHAPTER THREE

Involuntary Hospitalization and Treatment

Involuntary detention of a mentally ill person or other restriction of his freedom for non-criminal acts has long been practiced all over the world. In European countries and the United States, the procedures for such civil deprivation have been carried out under two main legal doctrines: 'police power' and '*parens patriae*'. Police power permits the state to take appropriate action, using force if necessary to safeguard the public at large. Thus, if a mentally ill person is considered dangerous he can be detained in a hospital against his will. The doctrine of *parens patriae,* which expresses the duty of the state to care for its citizens, permits the state to act on behalf of those citizens unable to care for themselves because of an infirmity such as a mental disability.[1]

CRITERIA

Certain criteria are usually mandated by law if a person is to be involuntarily hospitalized. Statutes vary from one country to another and from state to state. However, most secular laws have adopted similar basic principles to serve as a foundation for all criteria of commitment. These criteria include:

1. The presence of mental illness.
2. The risk of danger to self or others.
3. The inability to care for or provide basic personal needs.

As a matter of fact (3) is a variant of (2), since the inability to take care of basic personal needs constitutes a danger to self. Consequently, we are left with one principle (besides the presence of mental illness) on which involuntary hospitalization is based and that is 'risk of danger' to self or others.

Generally, each country defines explicitly the criteria to be met and what they mean. Unfortunately, terms like 'mental illness' or 'mentally ill' are often loosely defined. As a result, the responsibility for proper definition passes to the clinical judgment of the physician.

Certain countries have developed laws to permit the involuntary hospitalization of alcohol or drug addicts in addition to individuals with mental illnesses. But such decisions on substance-abusers are usually based on political considerations and are outside the scope of the ethics of medicine. For example, to force treatment on a drug abuser who has no interest in being treated is a political decision based on laws passed by a particular state. In these circumstances the physician functions mainly as an executor of these statutes.[2]

WHAT IS MENTAL ILLNESS?

The term mental illness is frequently used in legislating for hospital admission, discharge, competence, criminal responsibility and other issues in the context of forensic psychiatry. Yet, in spite of its obvious importance, many psychiatrists, possibly because of the legal arguments involved, only vaguely understand it. Psychiatry literature itself rarely uses the term 'mental illness' because it has no medical diagnostic significance. So it is hardly surprising that most physicians have difficulty with the term. In fact, neither the *Diagnostic and Statistical Manual IV* of the American Psychiatric Association nor *the International Classification of Disease* of the World Health Organization of the United Nations include the term 'mental illness' as a specific diagnosis in their classifications of diseases.

In this section we will try to standardize the term somewhat so that it can be used with a common understanding throughout this study.

Statutes around the world approach the task of defining mental illness in different ways. For example, some countries list particular psychiatric disorders, while others apply an impairment requirement that leaves the diagnosis to the professional judgment of the certifying physician. Most recently, the medico-legal community in the United States has adopted the following descriptions:

Definition of Mental illness

Mental illness is a severe *disturbance* in thinking, mood, perception, memory or cognition. This disturbance should cause an *impairment* of at least one of the following functions:

1. judgment
2. behavior
3. reality testing
4. facing ordinary demands of life.

One can see that the definition consists of two divisions or arms. One demands the presence of a 'disturbance' and the other the presence of an 'impairment'. Both must be present for mental illness to be identified.[3] If a person's condition satisfies one of the criteria of 'disturbance' and one of the criteria of 'impairment', he would be classified as mentally ill. If, on the other hand, the condition has all the criteria of 'disturbance' but none of 'impairment', he is not considered mentally ill; similarly, if he has all the criteria of 'impairment' but none of 'disturbance'.

Legal vs. Medical Approach to Civil Commitment

In the process of enacting any law to regulate involuntary hospitalization (otherwise known as civil commitment), there are two distinct and sometimes conflicting philosophical approaches that play a major part: the medical and the legal. The legal approach leans toward release, while the medical one toward admission. This is easily understood by analogy with a judge who, faced with little evidence to convict a defendant, would tend to let the defendant go free. The legal maxim says 'It is better to let 100 guilty individuals go free than to imprison one innocent man.' The medical approach takes the contrary line: when a physician is in doubt about a particular diagnosis, he will prefer to admit the patient in order to determine with more certainty whether the admission was justified or not. The maxim of the medical profession says, 'It is better to admit 100 persons who turn out to be healthy than to miss one sick individual.' Where the legal profession says 'when in doubt, release', the medical says 'when in doubt, admit.' This difference in basic philosophical approach between the two professions is the source of many conflicts in interpreting the civil commitment laws.

These are meant to strike a balance between two major duties, both of vital interest to the individual, namely the duty to treat the sick and the duty to preserve individual freedom of choice. They run smoothly with each other most of the time, when the person involved is alert, conscious and free from mental illness, but they come into direct conflict when the mental faculty is compromised.

To achieve a balance between those two principles is the essence of all civil commitment legislation. An individual who is ill is a person in need of treatment but he is also a person whose freedom of choice should be respected. Should he refuse treatment, this decision, even though it is not in his best interests, must be respected. As regards a mentally healthy individual, secular laws have no disagreement that the decision to accept or refuse treatment is to be left entirely to the person involved, regardless of the consequences to that person. This is not the case with mental illness, since the competence to make such a decision is brought into question by the nature of the illness. But how and where do we place the limits between the need for treatment and personal liberty for the mentally ill?

This question has been tackled in secular legal regimes by taking the 'risk of danger' as the criterion: if the patient is thought to be dangerous to himself or to others, he may be committed for treatment against his will. But applying this criterion in practice is problematic. How are we to evaluate 'risk of danger'? Do psychiatrists have the ability to assess such risk with sufficient accuracy to allow a fair balance between the need for treatment and protection on the one hand and preservation of personal liberty on the other? And what degree of accuracy is sufficient for the prediction of violent behavior when we know that psychiatrists may not be accurate in this type of prediction? If 'risk of danger' cannot be accurately assessed, then it must happen that a patient in need of treatment who refuses treatment will not be hospitalized against his will lest he be unjustly or improperly deprived of his right of personal choice in such matters. In this way, the right to treatment, promoted under the doctrine of *parens patriae*, is compromised in favor of the duty to preserve individual liberty.

Another criterion that may justify involuntary hospitalization is being so gravely disabled as to be incapable of self-care, and therefore in need of care and treatment. Under current secular law, a person not gravely disabled but in need of treatment will not require hospitalization but other protective services. The definition of gravely disabled varies, but encompasses a threat, to the person's life through inability to provide basic needs such as food, clothing or shelter.[4] Recently a rider was added to the laws of civil commitment indicating that the least restrictive environment should be resorted to first. For example, the patient would not be committed to a hospital if he could be treated in a day care center, and he would not be committed to a day care center if he could be treated on an outpatient basis, and so on.[5] But what of mentally ill patients who are not violent or 'dangerous' and who can meet some of their basic needs for themselves? Are such people to be left to fend for and tend themselves, if they refuse the proper regime of care and treatment they in fact need? This question is yet to be answered by secular law.

THE CONCEPT OF PATIENT CONSENT IN ISLAMIC LAW

There is a consensus among Islamic scholars that in ordinary circumstances, patient consent is mandatory before any medical treatment or procedure can take place.[6]

Islamic scholars have disagreed on whether obtaining consent frees the physician from liability for compensation in case of damage. There are two schools on this issue. The first states that the physician is liable for damages if he gives treatment without the consent of the patient. His liability is affirmed whether or not he performed the treatment by good medical standards. This opinion, which concurs with most secular laws, is the position of the major schools of Sunni *fiqh* – the Ḥanafī, Shāfiʿī, Mālikī and Ḥanbalī. It may be exemplified by this explicit comment in al-Disūqī: "If an unqualified physician, whether or not he performed the treatment to the proper professional standards, treated a patient without an accepted informed consent, that physician is fully liable."[7]

That opinion, though followed by the majority of Islamic legal scholars, was opposed by two famous and highly esteemed legal thinkers in Islamic jurisprudence. The first is Ibn Qayyim al-Jawziyya, a scholar of the Ḥanbalī school who, on this issue, deviated from the official position of his school to formulate his own opinion. He stated in his book *Iʿlām al-Muwaqqiʿīn:*

> A skilled physician who does the best he can in surgery and excises a part [organ or part of an organ] of a man, a young boy, or an insane person without obtaining his or his guardian's consent, or performed circumcision on a child without the consent of his father or guardian, is guilty of causing damage. Our colleagues say he is liable [for damages] because he performed a procedure without consent; had he done it with consent of the adult patient or consent of the child's or insane person's guardian, he would not have been liable for damages. I believe that he might not be liable at all (with or without consent), since he did it in good faith and his actions were meant for the welfare of the patient.[8]

The other scholar who took a similar position on liability was Ibn Ḥazm. He was well recognized in his field and had separated himself from the four main schools of jurisprudence and established his own school, which existed for hundreds of years. He made the following statement:

> On the issue of someone who amputated a hand used for eating, or extracted a painful or decayed tooth, without the consent of the patient, we should consider God's two statements in the Qur'an, the first in *Sūrah al-Mā'idah* (5:2) whose meaning is "help one another in virtue (*al-birr*) and God-fearing (*al-taqwā*), and do not help one another in sins (*al-ithm*) and enmities (*al-ʿudwān*)." This verse should be understood in contrast with the verse in *Sūrah al-Baqarah* (2:194) whose meaning is "and whoever assaults you, assault him in the same way as he assaulted you." So we should use these two verses in interpreting the action of the hand amputation or the extraction of the painful or decaying tooth. If it was done as treatment and the only treatment possible, there is no compensation for the lost hand and the physician should be praised, because the treatment was a good deed and the Prophet has ordered us to get treated.

Obviously if the action were interpreted as an assault, appropriate punishment would be in order. Ibn Ḥazm goes on to say that pain and suffering prevent people from praying to God and performing their daily duties in making a living, so treatment must be considered a good deed.[9]

We may conclude, from the statements made by Ibn Qayyim al-Jawziyya and Ibn Ḥazm, that treatment without the consent of patient or guardian is permissible in their opinion, and that the physician is not liable for damage incurred as long as he can prove that he acted in good faith. However, the contemporary practice under Islamic law takes the first position, that is, holding the physician liable for damages if he administered medicine or performed a procedure without the patient's consent.[10]

In contrast with most secular laws, there is no controversy in the Islamic tradition about the lawfulness of the physician treating someone without consent. The apparent consensus is that it is legal. The controversy is mainly regarding the liability for damages if some harm results to the person treated without consent. Under most secular laws, the patient can sue the physician for treating him without a consent regardless of the results of treatment, whether it leads to improvement in his quality of life or otherwise, since the action of treatment without consent is considered an assault. This reasoning holds in ordinary circumstances, that is, excluding emergency situations in which there is no time to secure consent before initiating treatment.

CLASSIFICATION OF PATIENT CONSENT IN ISLAMIC LAW

Islamic law has classified patient consent into several types according to the circumstances and conditions in the particular situation:

Restricted Consent

Such consent is given for a particular procedure or a particular medicine. It is considered the most formal kind of consent and there is no ambiguity about it nor any disagreement among legal scholars. For minors and patients who are incompetent to give it themselves, a restricted consent is taken from the patient's legal guardian.

Absolute Consent

Such consent is given to the physician by the patient to be treated with any medicine or procedure and does not specify the nature of the treatment. This would be the appropriate type of consent where the patient's knowledge of medicine is limited so that he lets the doctor decide on his behalf whatever regime of treatment is appropriate in his case. However, the jurists refused to allow this kind of consent to be absolutely unlimited. They required a particular consent for every medical procedure. Ibn Farhūn said that "the absolute consent is only taken for ordinary and common medical procedures."[11] The jurist al-Qurṭubī was asked about a man who hired a physician to treat pain in his knee. In his response he clarified that a proper consent must provide the patient sufficient information about the procedure and the instruments used, otherwise the consent and the patient–physician contract will not be valid.[12]

Implied Consent

This kind of consent is not declared verbally to the physician or put in written form, but is assumed to have been given through the special circumstances involved. The classical example given is if a physician while operating on a patient were to find another condition that required an excision or other particular action there and then in the operating room, he would assume the patient would consent to it, since it was being done for his welfare. Self-evidently, emergency procedures generally are included under this kind of consent. Non-emergency procedures in certain conditions might be included here, such as treating an insane person or a minor who cannot consent and the guardian or the next of kin cannot be found.[13]

Consent of a Minor

Minors cannot give their consent in any circumstances. The guardian, usually the father, must give consent on behalf of a minor. It is worth noting that none of the jurists has commented explicitly on what the consequences would be for a physician who violated the rules of consent and treated a minor without parental consent. The general position appears to be, with a few exceptions, that whoever treats a minor without proper consent will be liable for damages, regardless of the standard of care given. The question that arises is what consequences would a physician meet if he or she treated a child without consent, but with a good outcome, i.e.: no damage. Is the physician liable to a penalty for treating a child without parental consent even if no harm has resulted?

Another point of interest is that the age of consent, under Islamic law, is the age of sexual maturity, that is, around age fourteen to fifteen years for boys and age twelve to fourteen years for girls.[14]

RIGHT TO TREATMENT VS. DUTY TO PROTECT IN ISLAMIC LAW

Under secular law, the right of the mentally ill to treatment and care follows from the state's duty to protect its citizens when they consent to it. A mentally ill person's right to be treated is met when he requests treatment or accepts the offer of it. In normal circumstances his right to his personal liberty supersedes his right to treatment. The state's duty to protect its citizens is challenged when and if a mentally ill person is judged to be a threat to the community or to himself. Then, his right to treatment is raised as an issue and he is committed against his will to a treatment facility. His detention in such a facility should, by Donaldson's rule,[15] be accompanied by an offer of treatment. For, committing a patient to a hospital does not either automatically or usually guarantee his right to treatment, it only guarantees protection against the 'risk of danger' from the patient and an offer of treatment. The patient is still free to refuse this offer of treatment, as his involuntary status in the treatment facility does not mean that he can be treated involuntarily. According to many secular laws, another court order is necessary for him to be given medicine or be subjected to any form or regime of treatment against his will.

Under Islamic law, consent for minors or the mentally ill (insane) is given by their guardians. Without the consent of the guardian, no hospitalization or medical treatment can be rendered, except in an emergency. That there is a guardian implies legal incompetence on the part of the individual needing treatment; therefore, medical treatment will automatically be provided with the consent of the guardian. This in turn makes the right to treatment mandatory and the patient will be treated, even if he himself refuses.

The right to treatment is embedded in the duties assigned to the guardian. Shaykh Abū Zahrah, a well-known contemporary Islamic jurist, stresses this point explicitly:

> The guardian's duty to the mentally disabled is the same as that for a child, as both are facing life missing one important means of solving problems and making decisions, and that is an integrated mental faculty. It is through his mental competence that a man can defend himself, provide for himself and seek treatment.

He goes on to say that "the mentally ill person should not be left in the street, where he can be injured or harm other people, and he should not be left in indignity." In this argument the concept of 'risk of danger' is not considered relevant and is therefore unmentioned. The duty to care for and treat the mentally ill is the main moving force behind Islamic civil commitment laws.[16] We may conclude that, in Islamic law, the duty to care is more important than the duty to protect, and that the duty of the state to care should supersede individual liberty.

QUESTIONABLE COMMITMENT

Because of the relative inflexibility of secular law on the issue of individual liberty, many states have resorted to certain legal manoeuvres in order to overcome the legal difficulties that arise in many cases. For example, patients who do not meet commitment criteria but would benefit from hospitalization, would not be involuntarily hospitalized. In doubtful cases when the psychiatrist has reason to believe that the patient may be dangerous but is uncertain about this conclusion, it is our view that erring on the side of involuntary hospitalization would be justified. In these situations the psychiatrist should rely on his experience as a clinician to determine which course is in the patient's best interest, while allowing the court to temper clinical bias through legal scrutiny. For example, a patient in the emergency room in need of hospitalization may be informed that involuntary hospitalization is being considered for him. He may then agree to voluntary admission in order to be able to sign out shortly thereafter. To avoid this kind of eventuality, patients who are likely to sign out of the hospital prematurely should be considered for involuntary hospitalization from the outset, even though this is not consistent with the current policy of the least restrictive alternative.

Under the Islamic legal system, such twists and turns within the law are not necessary; involuntary hospitalization will not require a specific level of 'risk of danger' or grave disability, the need for hospital care and treatment will be enough justification for admission. In one example, a famous Islamic jurist gave this ruling in the case of a mentally ill woman who needed treatment for head lice: "It is acceptable to treat an insane woman for head lice without consent, if her next of kin is not available." The treatment was carried out without formal consent because in this case implied consent sufficed.[17] It is clear from the circumstances of this case that the woman's condition did not constitute an emergency, and 'risk of danger' to herself or others was not an issue. Yet the jurist determined that the right to treatment takes precedence, even in the absence of a guardian. This example corroborates the argument that, at least according to some jurists, even ordinary treatment procedures are permissible for insane and legally incompetent people without consent.

CHAPTER FOUR

Mental Competencies

WHAT IS MENTAL COMPETENCE

Competence is a capacity or a potential for mental functioning, required in a decision-specific manner, to understand and carry out decision-making. Competence is always presumed; its absence or inactivity has to be affirmed by a court. Incompetence means that a mental illness is causing a defect in reasoning or judgment relevant to a particular matter.

The corresponding term in Islamic law, *ahlīyah*, is better translated as 'eligibility', a term that covers eligibility as to rights or *entitlement*, and eligibility as to duties or *responsibility*. Islamic law divides *ahlīyah* into two branches:

1. Competence of entitlement, *ahlīyat al-wujūb*.
2. Competence of performance, *ahlīyat al-adā'*.

COMPETENCE OF ENTITLEMENT

Competence of entitlement means eligibility or responsibility in respect of rights and duties which belong to a person irrespective of level of intelligence or mental function. The collective contract to assure this entitlement of persons as persons is indicated in the use of the term *dhimmah*.[1] For example, the fetus inside his mother's womb is eligible to receive his inheritance, to carry his father's name, be the subject of a will, receive appropriate medical care, and so on. On the responsibilities side, *ahlīyat al-wujūb* imposes on the individual, regardless of his level of understanding thereof, such duties as payment of taxes in the form of zakah, and of the bloodwit due from the family of one convicted of homicide or manslaughter. While the subject of fundamental recognition of a person as a person may not be directly related to competence, it is addressed under that head in Islamic literature.

COMPETENCE OF PERFORMANCE

The definition of 'competence of performance' in Islamic law is like that of mental competence. It is the person's ability to perform a task in a legally accepted way, his fitness for proper personal interactions so that these interactions affirm certain rights for himself or others. These interactions include verbal and non-verbal communication, together with sufficient understanding of specific types of interaction in such a way that they will hold legally. Under Islamic law every individual who reaches adulthood is presumed to be mentally competent in all relevant respects unless declared not to be so according to legally accepted arguments, or competence is contested and its absence proven. Adulthood is generally understood to begin when puberty ends, although there are differences of detail on this among jurists between and within the different schools.

CIVIL RESPONSIBILITY AND LIABILITY

Islamic law distinguishes between mental competence and civil responsibility. When a person is recognized as competent to make a commercial deal, this holds true whether he has made a deal or not. So competence is a characteristic of the person and is not related to any particular event. On the other hand, personal responsibility or liability is not a constant characteristic but is directly related to events, and attaches to the person involved in those events for which, if they lead to personal injury or damage to property, he may be held responsible. Whether he was competent and aware, or actually intended to cause damage is not an issue with regard to holding him responsible for the action. Being responsible involves liability to provide compensation to an injured party. The competence, or intention, of the person involved is considered a factor affecting outcome only in criminal cases, when an incompetent person is not eligible for punishment. The same is true for acts done unintentionally.[2]

It is important to note that compensation for damages has a

special characteristic in Islamic law. If there is property damage, compensation is the responsibility of the person who caused the damage. This responsibility does not go beyond the person who caused the damage, so if a young child caused damage intentionally or otherwise, and by virtue of his age he is not criminally responsible, the compensation should be paid from his own money, not from his parent or guardian's. If the child has no money of his own, the compensation is held as a debt against him until it can be paid.

If the damage is personal injury severe enough to cause unintentional death (or 'manslaughter') as it is called in secular law, the compensation or bloodwit is not the responsibility of the one who committed the manslaughter; it should be paid by his family and tribe, even if he has enough money of his own to cover it.[3]

AGE AND MENTAL COMPETENCE

A child is not generally considered to have full mental competence until he is about seven years of age. This is an arbitrary figure for what is legally termed the 'age of recognition'. Before that age the child is not culpable in law. Also, while he enjoys competence of entitlement, he is not required to fulfill any duties to others or perform religious rites. The child at this age is under full guardianship and all legal and commercial interactions are conducted through his legal guardian. The strictly religious taxes like zakah have to be paid from his own money according to the Shāfiʿī, Ḥanbalī and Mālikī schools; the Ḥanafī school, however, considers that a child before the age of recognition is not responsible even for that.[4]

The age of recognition is when the child is able to understand the meaning of the words used in commercial contracts, like 'sell' and 'buy'. He is expected to recognize the difference and the relationship between what is said and what is done, and between right and wrong. Scholars chose the age of seven as the age of recognition for more than one reason. First, the Prophet identified the seventh year as the age when children must pray, and sleep in separate beds.[5] Second, most children at this age are in fact able to understand some aspects of commercial interactions and the binding quality of verbal statements. At age of recognition, the child is judged as mentally competent to deal only with certain types of interactions, which are classified in three categories:

1. Acts that do not legally require the approval of his guardian: these acts are judged to be in the interests of his person and may not be against his interests. They include acceptance of gifts, charity or wills. He may perform work for others and accept fees; although the guardian's approval is preferred for that, it is not mandatory.

2. Transactions that are invalid even with the approval of the guardian: those that are judged to cause a loss or depreciation of wealth, whether for a good cause or otherwise. For example, a child at age of recognition cannot give gifts or charity, or write a will. In certain circumstances, a judge (but not the guardian) may allow some money to be loaned out as lending keeps money from being wasted. Under the Shāfiʿī school, a will written by a child at age of recognition is valid if it serves charitable or other righteous purposes. The Ḥanafī school, however, disallows this.[6]

3. Transactions are valid only if they are approved by the legal guardian, except those that are difficult to judge as being in the interest of the recognizing child, like selling and investing, or working for fees, or getting married (marriage of minors at any age is legal under Islamic law, whether consummated or not.) This is the rule under the Ḥanafī school. The Shāfiʿī school does not recognize any contract at this age whether approved by the guardian or not.[7]

ADULTHOOD IN ISLAMIC LAW

The concept of adulthood as it is understood in the secular literature does not exist in Islamic law. Two different terms are used for adulthood. The first, *bulūgh* (literally, 'arrival', 'attainment'), is used in Islamic law to denote attainment of full sexual maturity, when most of the responsibilities of an adult are expected legally. A person is then considered fully responsible for his actions, unless he is known to be not competent for a particular action. It is the age when punishment for any legal violation is administered and when the person is obliged to perform all his religious duties towards God and his fellow men. The proof for this rule is derived from the Qur'an and the Prophet's teachings. In the Qur'an it is stated, "those who have not reached sexual maturity [*lam yablughū*] . . . " (24:58), and "when your children reach sexual maturity [*idhā balagha*], they should take permission . . . " (24:59). The Prophet stated that "The pen is lifted [that is, there is no culpability] for the child until he reaches puberty [*ḥattā yaḥluma*], and for the insane until he recovers, and for the sleeping person until he wakes."[8] The Prophet also imposed taxes on those eligible when they reached sexual maturity. If puberty is delayed or not evident, the age of culpability will not exceed fifteen.

It is important to note that sexual maturity is referred to by some authors as puberty. The terms puberty and sexual maturity appear to be used more or less interchangeably but we believe that the term sexual maturity is more reflective of the meaning. The caliph ʿUmar identified those youths who can shave as having reached maturity, and this usually happens later in puberty.

The other term used in Islamic law to denote adulthood is *rushd* (literally, 'guidance'). That is the time when a person is guided by virtue of his age and wisdom to recognize his own best interests. It is at this age when a minor is expected to take full charge of his money. This age, according to the Ḥanafī school, is twenty-five years. According to other schools, it is not judged by age at all but by individual merit.

COMPETENCE TO MARRY AND DIVORCE

Under secular law, a certain level of mental competence is usually required for a marriage to take place. This level may not be very high but the persons involved must understand the nature of marriage, the marital relationship and the duties and obligations of that union.

Under Islamic law, the legality of a marriage contract is not affected by age or level of competence. It must be either approved or actually carried out by the guardian if either partner is too young or mentally incompetent. For a minor below the age of recognition, the marriage contract cannot be valid legally through his own statement or action, but only through that of his guardian. Above the age of seven and before completion of puberty, a boy can carry out a marriage contract on his own but requires the approval of his guardian to make it binding. After puberty, a man can make such a contract on his own. According to the majority of Islamic law schools, women marrying for the first time require the approval of their guardian at any age.[9] A mentally incompetent person can marry through his guardian's authority. Divorce, on the other hand, cannot be carried out through another person, i.e. the guardian, according to the more popular schools. It requires full mental competence and is subject to more complicated regulations.

COMPETENCE TO MAKE A CONTRACT

Sanctity of contracts is essential for the dealings of daily life. Secular law lays down certain criteria for competence to make a contract that include understanding the nature, term and effect of the particular transaction. Any lack of understanding must be due to an illness and not to ignorance or lack of sophistication.

Islamic law does not directly specify criteria for mental competence to make a contract. It does, nevertheless, address the issue. It requires different criteria and sets limits that vary with the type of disorder, mental state, biological state and circumstances involved. For example, it explicitly describes the different conditions under which a minor is considered competent. It also gives a particular view on contracts signed by the insane. It has addressed the same issues regarding the mentally retarded with some modified criteria of competence. Competence to write a will is conceived in a way unique to Islamic law. Competence to handle one's own money is treated as a distinct subject. It is therefore difficult to present the subject of competence to make contracts as a single entity. It is discussed under the following headings:

1. *Competence of minors to make contracts*

Minors below the age of seven cannot be involved in any kind of contract. Above the age of seven, they may do so with the consent of the guardian, unless the contract does not require them to risk money or property. They can act independently after puberty.

2. *Competence of the Mentally Deficient to Make Contracts*

Mental retardation and dementia are addressed by Islamic scholars under the same legal term, *ʿatah* (see above, p.22) which literally means 'mental deficiency' and is characterized by variation between normal and abnormal mental function, or insanity.[10]

The rules, in respect of competence to make competence, for those who are mentally deficient are the same as those for the child at the age of recognition. They are able to carry out certain contracts that do not put their wealth at risk and they can enter risk-taking contracts with approval from their guardian. They are forbidden to enter contracts that involve monetary gifts or donations, regardless of the desire of their guardian.[11]

A person identified as retarded or suffering dementia to a certain level has the right to deputize someone in his place. He can also assume the function of a deputy for others. This function must, however, be for duties in which his competence is assumed. These duties may include transactions like divorcing a wife and selling and buying property. When such a person is acting on behalf of others with their formal approval to sell or buy, he cannot be held liable for any defect or error in the transaction. For example, he is not expected to pay for defective or undelivered merchandise. That is the responsibility of the person for whom he is deputizing.[12]

3. *Competence of the Insane to Make Contracts*

Under Islamic law the insane are, as a general rule, considered legally incompetent to make a contract. Insanity, however, is known to vary in intensity and duration and that rule is therefore applied to cover the occasions when a person is known to be insane. During periods of remission or recovery, he is considered to be competent and his contract is binding. Islamic literature does identify partial insanity. It would therefore follow that competence must be specified according to what level of mental functioning is required to make a specific decision. The criteria for mental incompetence to carry out a specific act or transaction have not, to date, been directly addressed in the Islamic literature. These criteria, or similar issues, however, have been discussed briefly in regard to *ʿatah*. Since, according to many jurists, the rules and legal arguments applied to those suffering mental deficiency also apply to the insane, it is probably legitimate to extrapolate the same criteria for both.

Contemporary psychiatry has modified the understanding and treatment of mental illness: what is described as partial insanity or transient psychosis is the rule rather than the exception among individuals recognized as insane. It follows that more detailed studies to update the descriptions and criteria of mental competence in Islamic jurisprudence will be necessary.

COMPETENCE TO SIGN INTO A HOSPITAL OR INSTITUTION

Voluntary patients must be competent to sign into a hospital or institution. In order to fulfill that requirement, the person need not necessarily understand the implications of the hospitalization, it is enough that he does not object to the process of hospitalization or institutionalization. This low level of competence is accepted because the institutionalization is presumed to be for the good of the patient. If the patient refuses, the procedures governing involuntary hospitalization are followed. This is the case under most secular law. In Islamic law, the best interests of the patient take precedence, if need be, over personal liberty or right to refuse treatment. The competence necessary to sign into an institution is either the patient's own willingness to do so or, in the event of refusal, it becomes the duty of his guardian, or of the state if no guardian is available to commit the patient for appropriate hospital care.

COMPETENCE TO MAKE A WILL

It has been recognized throughout history that a mentally incompetent person cannot make a valid will. Increased sophistication in forensic issues in psychiatry in recent times has led to the requirement that certain criteria be met before the would-be testator is considered legally incompetent to make a will. No longer does the presence of mental illness of itself prevent a person from making a legally valid will. Under most popular laws, the testator is required to understand the following:

1. The nature of the will or bequest and its meaning, as a means of disposition of his wealth and property after death.

2. The extent of the wealth and property being disposed of. This might not mean knowing every penny, but should be broadly accurate.

3. Who are the natural heirs or expected recipients of his wealth and property, i.e. knowing those parties who would be the usual beneficiaries, such as relatives, friends, servants and charities.

4. The testator should understand and appreciate the effect of the will on others. (This criterion is not required in many countries.)

5. The testator should not be suffering from delusion.

The above provide the understanding that mental illness by itself, unless it is associated with delusion and interferes with any of the above criteria, would not affect a person's competence to make a will.[13]

In Islamic law there are two main limitations to writing a will that are not related to competence:

1. The will cannot involve a donation in excess of one-third of the whole wealth of the testator.

2. The testator cannot dispose his wealth among his heirs as he pleases. Rather, each natural heir will get his prescribed share (regardless of the wishes of the testator) according to the laws of inheritance as they are written in the Qur'an. It follows that the only disputable portion will be the one-third that it is allowed to bequeath.

Islamic law clearly states that mental competence is required for making a legally valid will. It does not, however, specify criteria for that competence. It refers to mental incompetence as insanity in a generalized way. As insanity has been described in different grades and intensities with, for each, a rule appropriate to the action or transaction in question, the five criteria set out above, subject to the two limitations indicated, could be adapted into Islamic law.

Islamic jurists have discussed many details in respect of changes in the mental competence of the testator after the writing of the will, with variations in the rulings given by different scholars. Al-Kāsānī has stated that "if mental incompetence, i.e. insanity, occurs after the writing of the will, the document will not be valid because it is not a permanent contract, and it so remains if the person does not recover from the state of insanity before death." Ibn ᶜĀbidīn seconds that opinion, adding that the document is invalid if the state of insanity lasts longer then six months.[14] By contrast, jurists of the Mālikī school state that the will should remain valid because the insane person cannot make a will unless he is in remission or has recovered. It has also been argued that the will is a valid document even after death, so it cannot be invalidated by a mental illness.[15] The law in Egypt invalidates the will if the testator became insane after making it and did not recover before death.[16]

UNDUE INFLUENCE

Undue influence is defined as pressure applied unfairly with the intent of benefiting the person who exercised the influence.

A human approaching death is vulnerable. It is not unusual for a dying person to become over-attached to, and easily influenced by, the care-givers immediately near about him. If this should lead him to change his will to include them as beneficiaries, it would be considered undue influence. The burden is on the fiduciaries to prove undue influence. If they are able to provide the evidence for it, the change in the will will be invalidated.

This type of influence has long been recognized in Muslim law. It is clearly stated that any type of transaction carried out during an illness that leads to death will be questionable. If a dying person sold property to one of his natural heirs, the transaction would be invalidated because a natural heir cannot benefit from a will for any amount in excess of his legal share, as prescribed in the Shariᶜah. If the transaction involved a person who is not a natural heir, such as selling property to a stranger, that kind of transaction would be valid in the framework of a will provided that the value of the property sold does not exceed a third of the disposable whole.

As in secular law, the burden of proof is on the fiduciaries. In Islamic law, however, the fiduciary does not have to prove undue influence, only that the particular transaction was carried out during the illness that led to death.[17]

The kind of transaction in question need not have to do with only selling and buying; it can be any kind of transaction that directly or indirectly affects the outcome of the will. For example, the act of divorce will not be valid for the purpose of inheritance, if it is done during an illness followed by death. In other words, the divorce has legally taken place as a means to end the marriage, but the ex-wife will keep her right to her share of the inheritance as if she were still married to the deceased. The thinking behind this ruling is the assumption that any decision taken during an illness that was followed by death could have been caused by undue influence of relatives on the deceased, or an ill-intention of the deceased to deprive his wife of her due inheritance by divorcing her at the end of his life.

COMPETENCE TO DEAL WITH ONE'S WEALTH

We mentioned before that the age of maturity in Islamic law, namely, completion of puberty, does not have the same meaning as does, in secular law, the age of competence to deal with one's own financial affairs. Although no specific age has been given by most jurists, they have acknowledged that the age of maturity may or may not be accompanied by *rushd* which, in this context, means financial competence. So a minor who reaches sexual maturity (puberty), if judged to have attained *rushd*, will be entitled to his wealth and to deal with it according to his wishes. If, however, he is judged to be not competent, he will continue under guardianship. Abū Ḥanīfah indicated that *rushd* should not exceed the age of twenty-five in the absence of mental illness. The Ḥanafī school adds that even if *rushd* were not attained by the age of twenty-five, the guardianship should discontinue and the individual take charge of his own affairs, financial and otherwise, unless mental incompetence is established.[18]

One school of Islamic law that endured some centuries but now has few followers, the Ẓāhirī, does not accept the concept of *rushd* or age of financial competence, so it allows a person who has reached the age of sexual maturity to handle his money without looking into how it will be spent.[19]

Most schools of Islamic *fiqh* have regarded *rushd* as essential before a person can take charge of his own financial affairs, regardless of age or the presence or absence of mental illness. In fact, when any individual at any age starts behaving irresponsibly and squandering his money, he can be declared incompetent to deal with his money and a guardian will be appointed for that purpose. An adult who has been declared incompetent to deal with his own financial affairs in the absence of mental illness is termed *safīh*. The term (from *safah*, literally 'lightness of weight and movement') denotes 'recklessness', or 'folly' (see above, p.21).[20] Some scholars defined it as a lightness of mental faculty that, despite freedom from mental illness, makes the individual deal with his money in a way that is not acceptable to right-minded or reasonable people. Others defined it as the state in which, despite health of mind, a person exposes wealth (i.e. over-spends or over-risks) in a way unacceptable in Islamic law or to a Muslim of sound mind. It was also defined as a sort of arrogant nonchalance that overwhelmed a sound mind so that the mind was not used.[21]

In order to understand how the concept of *safīh* was applied, we need to elaborate on the concept of *rushd*. In its technical use, it is defined as "the proper behavior regarding money and religion and spending for good causes and causes acceptable by God." The Shāfiʿī school defines it as "the proper behavior of the individual with God and his money." According to the last definition, a person who is not behaving properly in respect of the teachings of Islam is included in the definition of *safīh*, which could mean depriving religiously non-observant people of control of their financial affairs. Some jurists would not allow the testimony of a *safīh* in court and would prevent him from deputizing for others.[22] This position, however, is not supported by some jurists, such as al-Ṣafadī and al-Thawrī, who believe that there is no relationship between a person's competence to deal with money and his level of religious observance.[23]

CRITERIA OF FINANCIAL COMPETENCE

There is disagreement among Islamic legal schools on whether *rushd* is a requirement for one to take charge of one's wealth. They differ in their definition and criteria of competence. The Shāfiʿī school holds that irresponsibility in spending can only be termed *safah* when it is overspending on what is forbidden in Islamic law. Spending the money for good causes cannot be called overspending, regardless of the amount spent. The Ḥanafī school takes a different position. It considers that any kind of overspending and waste merits the designation of *safīh*, that waste is waste even if it is spent on building mosques and hospitals. The difference between the two schools is based on their views of the rationale behind restricting a *safīh's* right to deal with his financial affairs. The Shāfiʿī view sees the measure as punishment for a wasteful, irresponsible spendthrift; whereas money dispensed in charitable donations is a good deed and not liable to punishment. The Ḥanafī view sees the measures as protecting the person and his wealth from his weakness.

Spending money on wining and dining, gambling or on what is considered a wasteful hobby such as buying a large number of birds, are all undisputed conditions for declaring a person *safīh*. Such a ruling can be associated with the concept of protecting the human rights of others; squandering one's money can affect immediate relatives and future heirs.[24]

It is important to note that the Ḥanafī school only recognizes a *safah* ruling for those who have never attained financial competence. In other words, it does not permit the ruling on adults with financial competence, as this kind of competence cannot be lost without a clear indication of mental illness. So adults who have never been declared financially incompetent cannot lose financial competence for reason of *safah*. However, the majority of jurists do not follow the Ḥanafī line on this issue, and can declare a sane adult as 'financially incompetent', even if he had been known to be competent all his life before.

SPECIAL INTERDICTION OR *ḤAJR*

The term *ḥajr* (from *ḥajara*, literally meaning to 'hinder' or 'restrict access to' and so 'forbid') was used by the Islamic jurists to denote an interdiction upon an individual to prevent his dealing with some or all interpersonal transactions. This procedure is usually undertaken when the individual is declared to be partially or wholly incompetent. The precise definition of *ḥajr* varies according to different schools of Islamic jurisprudence, and there are also some differences among schools in identifying the circumstances requiring this procedure and how it is applied.

According to the Ḥanafī school, *ḥajr* is a particular act which prevents a person from conducting or effecting particular transactions. For example, a minor may be prevented from spending his money or an incompetent may be prevented from making a big gift or from divorcing his wife. The judge or the court will assign a guardian to handle the personal affairs of the individual under the *ḥajr* restriction according to his best interests. The Ḥanafī school excludes certain types of transaction from the guardian's authority. It considers any transaction (such as receiving a gift) that cannot be manipulated to harm the interests of the person as valid regardless of the position of the guardian on the matter. Behavior that might or might not be considered beneficial, such as selling or buying, should be approved by the guardian. The determinant of what kind of transaction needs the approval of the guardian is the degree or level of mental competence in question.

The person under *ḥajr* restriction is also considered as not responsible for his criminal actions, and so cannot receive criminal punishment. However, he is not protected from civil liability.

The Mālikī school defines *ḥajr* as a ruling which prevents a person from executing actions and transactions beyond his (mental) ability or competence. The guardian should approve all commercial and other major transactions but cannot approve a donation or a gift that exceeds one-third of the whole wealth of his ward.

The Shāfiʿī school defined *ḥajr* as preventing a person from dealing with money. This is a very precise statement and clearly restricts the procedure to monetary transactions, so that other transactions such as marriage, divorce, confession, deputizing for non-commercial purposes and matters of worship, are not restricted. However, the *ḥajr* is not limited in that way for the insane and minors, and will be applied to any action or transaction of vital interest to them.

The Ḥanbalī school also restricts *ḥajr* to monetary matters, including in the definition any decision to do with material possessions not paid for, or under dispute.

Ḥajr can be ruled for a variety of reasons, the most common of which is mental incompetence. However, this is by no means the only reason. The bankrupt and the reckless (*safīh*) are included in this ruling. It can also be applied to any person who is so sick that his death is anticipated. According to the Mālikī school, a sick person may have the privilege of donating or giving away no more than one-third of his total disposable wealth. A wife is under partial *ḥajr*, in that she cannot give away more then one-third of her money without the approval of her husband.[25]

THE GUARDIAN

When a *ḥajr* ruling is applied, a guardian must be appointed. The concept of guardian has been extensively studied in Islamic law. Some issues are agreed by consensus, while others vary slightly according to school of thought.

According to the Ḥanafī school, the guardian assigned should be the father; and the father will choose someone to be guardian after his death. The third in line will be the grandfather, then whomever the grandfather chooses. Afterwards, no priority is given and the choice is left to the judge. The mother cannot take the role of guardian of her child's money. Also if the mother dies, the child's inheritance (if he is still a minor or mentally incompetent) cannot be under the control of anyone but his father or the line of guardians in the order just given.

Guardianship over personal matters such as marriage, divorce and consent for hospitalization follows a different line. It starts with the closest relatives, then the relatives by marriage, then the judicial and the executive systems, that is, the judge or the governor. The closest relative is the son, then the grandson, then the father, then the grandfathers, then brothers, and so on.

The Shāfiʿī school assigns priority of guardianship to the father, then the grandfathers; and then to whoever the father or grandfathers choose. That is in contrast to the Ḥanafī school which puts the father's choice ahead of the grandfather's. Also, the Shāfiʿī school allows the mother to be a guardian in the absence of the father and the grandfather, if she has proved to be efficient. The older male relatives, like the uncles, are still expected to share in guidance and discipline in addition to their responsibility in financial support.

The Mālikī school gives priority to the father. Next is the father's choice among relatives or friends, then any other person the father chooses, and so on. If there was no particular choice made by the father or the next guardian, the judge will assign one of his choice.

The Ḥanafī school stipulates that the guardian in charge of financial matters may not be the same person as the one in charge of personal ones. The only person who can be a guardian for both matters is the father, unless he has deputed authority to a person of his choice to deal with his child's money. The non-father guardian cannot do that. He is authorized to make decisions for the minor or the mentally incompetent on personal matters only. He can keep the incompetent person's money in the form of savings but nothing else unless specifically authorized to do so by the father before his death.

The Ḥanbalī school agrees on giving the priority of guardianship to the father or someone of the father's choice only; not the grandfather or any other relative. The mother cannot be a guardian. The Ḥanbalī school leaves the decision to the judge if the father made no particular choice of guardian.[26]

CAN THE GUARDIAN CARRY OUT COMMERCIAL TRANSACTIONS?

The Islamic schools of jurisprudence agree on basic principles; they disagree on minor details. The guardian usually has full authority to make decisions of a personal nature on behalf of the ward. However, he is not automatically able to carry out business transactions on his ward's behalf. As a general rule, if the guardian happens to be the father he is permitted to carry on business transactions according to his judgment. A non-father guardian can do some commercial transactions if they are thought to be in the best interests of the person in question. These actions, however, are to be approved by the judge before being considered valid. By the same token, donations to charity are accepted through the guardian only under special conditions and are not to exceed one-third of the ward's whole wealth.

All Islamic jurists are strict in demanding honesty and integrity on the part of the guardian. This demand is required even if the guardian assigned is the father.[27]

COMPETENCE TO BE EXECUTED

While there is a clear consensus about the non-responsibility of an insane person for a crime committed during the period of his insanity, opinion varies if an individual commits a crime in a clear mental state and then becomes seriously mentally ill after conviction. According to the Shāfiʿī and Ḥanbalī schools, the execution should still be carried out because he was sane when he committed the crime.

The Ḥanafī school has looked at the matter more carefully, recognizing the importance of the formal trial in deciding this matter. It argued that the point at which insanity has to be evaluated is during the trial. If the offender was convicted without the appearance of insanity, he is expected to be handed over to the family of the victim immediately afterwards. If he was handed over in a sane condition, it is the family's decision to execute him or not if insanity ensues.

The Mālikī school is divided on the issue. Imām Mālik thinks a convicted insane person should be kept in custody until he recovers and then be executed when his illness is in remission. Ibn al-Fawāz adds that if, due to the seriousness of the illness, his recovery is not expected, he should give the bloodwit from his own wealth because according to this jurist no insane person would be executed.[28] Another jurist named Mughira believed that the decision should be given entirely to the family of the victim; it would be up to them to let him live or have him executed but they cannot accept compensation in lieu.[29] Al-Lakhmī, however, believed that the family of the victim have the choice to have the offender executed or set free, or to accept bloodwit.[30]

CHAPTER FIVE

Islamic Family Laws in Forensic Psychiatry

Islamic jurists have given family laws a good deal of attention and long chapters in the legal texts are devoted to the subject. Scholars have recognized issues where these laws relate to the mental state of the individual and addressed these to the best of their ability, considering the limited knowledge of psychiatry in earlier times.

The association between family laws and mental health lies in the term 'family'. A psychiatric condition or disorder can rarely be identified and properly evaluated without a good look at the family. Family laws deal with marriage, divorce and child custody. Problems of child abuse, although considered a family matter, are addressed separately because of their importance and the frequent involvement of non-family members. We will therefore limit the discussion here to three areas – marriage, divorce and child custody.

MARRIAGE

The marital contract can be annulled by the wife in certain circumstances, including insanity of the husband. The man has the right to divorce without giving particular reasons whereas the wife's choice of annulment is detailed differently according to the school of jurisprudence.

The Mālikī school gives the choice of annulment to the wife if insanity was present at the time of making the contract. This is valid whether the wife knew about it beforehand or not. If insanity develops after the marriage contract, the wife has no right to annulment. The Shāfiʿī and Ḥanbalī schools rule that if the wife knew about the presence of insanity at the time of the marriage contract, she has no choice or right to break the contract later. The Ḥanafī school has taken a completely different position. It rules that the wife has no choice to annul the marriage for reasons of insanity in any circumstances. A judge can rule for the wife to be divorced according to her wishes only if she can prove that serious harm is being done to her in the marriage. This would be grounds for separation and divorce also under the Mālikī rule. Under these circumstances, the wife, however will be granted no financial rights from the husband. The Ḥanafī, Ḥanbalī and Shāfiʿī school do not consider physical abuse of a wife a ground for divorce; instead, they would decree criminal punishment against the husband if his abusive behavior persists.[1]

DIVORCE

Although mental competence does not constitute a major issue in getting married, it does in getting divorced The level of mental competence which qualifies a man to divorce his wife is not limited to the presence or absence of mental illness. It goes beyond that to include freedom from intoxicating substances, and his state of temper.

The special attention Islamic scholars have given to mental health issues in relation to divorce is attributed to several reasons. Some are clearly understandable in light of the gravity of divorce itself. The Islamic ethos is protective of family unity, and therefore Islamic legal thinking tries to limit it to the extent possible. Another reason might be the fact that divorce is a prerogative of the husband only. He has full power and authority in law to divorce his wife without reason or excuse. We stress the phrase 'in law' here to point out that even if a man divorces his wife for an unfair reason, the divorce is legally valid. That does not mean that the religion condones it: a man who threatens his wife unjustly by divorce or otherwise is committing a transgression and can expect the punishment of God. Since divorce is left to the man to decide, the law places many conditions on that power of decision. One of them is well-identified mental competence.

Another reason for strictness about mental state lies in the oral tradition of the culture. In this tradition, the word spoken was a bond, a firm pledge: utterance of the words "You are divorced" three times by the husband, with the intention of divorce, at once validates the divorce. This, together with the fact that a husband can return his wife no later than after pronouncing divorce the second time, means they cannot get back together unless she marries another man and in turn is divorced by him. So we can see the seriousness of the verbal declaration of divorce, for it can be practically irreversible. The Prophet is quoted as saying: "Three matters, if said seriously, are serious and if joked about, are serious – marriage, divorce and setting a slave free." Some scholars have taken that saying to rule that divorce, even if said jokingly, is valid.[2]

The mental fitness of the man to pronounce divorce will be addressed under the following headings: maturity, mental illness, voluntary or involuntary intoxication, and rage.

Maturity

The question of the age of the husband is now probably one of academic interest only. Most Islamic countries currently do not permit children below the age of puberty to get married. This law is made on the authority of the state. Under the authority of the Shariʿah, however, children at any age can get married through the power of their guardians.

The Ḥanafī school of jurisprudence takes the ruling of the majority of the jurists, that makes a child incompetent to divorce until he reaches the age of puberty, whether or not he can recognize the meaning of divorce before then. The Ḥanbalī school holds that a child, even below that age, often can divorce his wife if he is able to understand what divorce means and what consequences it carries.[3]

Mental Illness

There is consensus among all schools that a mentally ill person recognized as insane cannot be competent to decide on a divorce. The insanity rule is also applied to the mentally retarded, to those in a delirious state for whatever reason, or under the effect of legally acquired drugs. The jurists, however, have not identified a test for judging the severity of the mental defect that would qualify a person as incompetent to divorce. It is expected that this will be studied and standardized by contemporary religious scholars in association with qualified psychiatrists.[4]

The Effect of Alcohol and Drugs

Legal systems the world over do not recognize having taken an intoxicating drug as an excuse for committing a crime. A person is responsible for his actions while voluntarily using these substances. The fact that the person was not aware of his actions during the intoxication cannot be grounds for freeing him of responsibility for his actions. That is understandable for criminal acts; however, under Islamic law a pronouncement of divorce is subject to the same rule.

Islamic law views the use of alcohol and, by analogy, any illicit drugs as a major sin, which makes the issue more complicated. That, compounded by the fact that the verbal utterance of divorce carries as much weight as the written statement, and that a divorce can be an irreversible process once declared a third time, means the couple cannot reunite again even if the divorce was uttered minutes earlier. Regretting a pronounced divorce cannot cancel its legal effect.

Consuming alcohol is not only prohibited under Islamic law but carries with it two kinds of punishment. One is termed a *ḥadd*, a punishment determined by God in the Qur'an or by His Messenger, and in this case it is eighty lashes, according to the opinion of the majority of jurists. The other punishment is stipulated by the state authorities and can vary according to what the ruler considers proper at the time. According to the Ḥanafī school, the *ḥadd* is only applicable to a certain state and degree of drunkenness: if the severity of drunkenness is such that the drunk person was unable to distinguish the earth from the sky, or unable to tell the difference between a man and a woman. Obviously this is a clearly verified test of mental incompetence, indicating seriously impaired mental function. However, the majority of Islamic jurists, in spite of their acknowledgment of mental incompetence of that severity, have decided that a drunken man at any level of consciousness or mental impairment, even if it is worse than the one just described, who utters a statement to the effect that his wife is divorced, will have a valid divorce which would be irreversible if it was the third declaration. They have based their reasons on the fact that if the divorce of the wife is regretted, it will be a punishment for the man for consuming a forbidden substance. The argument presented by some that this might be an unfair punishment because it affects the innocent (wife and children), was refuted by the argument that a man who gets drunk is not worth living with.

There were two significant opinions in Islamic legal history which rejected the rule that the decision of an incompetent person that unfairly affects others is nonetheless valid. The opinions were held by al-Farrāz and Abū al-Ḥasan al-Karkhī.[5] Both asserted that if a man pronounces divorce while under the influence of alcohol, even mildly so, the divorce will not be valid unless he maintains the decision when sober. The lenient view of these two scholars is now accepted in many Islamic countries which therefore reject the majority opinion. In Saudi Arabia as well as in Egypt, for example, divorce pronounced while intoxicated is not valid.[6]

Rage

The Islamic jurists gave particular attention to 'rage' and its effect on state of mind. They recognized that frequent marital conflict can provoke anger and a rage reaction may take place. The man may rant and rave, and curse, and decide to divorce his wife on the spur of the moment. He will more than likely change his mind and regret what he has done when the crisis is over. Simply changing one's mind about a decision as serious as divorce is not enough to cancel its effects, especially if it is a third and therefore irreversible divorce. Jurists therefore designed criteria to identify what is meant by rage and what level of anger constitutes a state of rage.

Generally speaking, rage is divided into three levels. There is no disagreement on the role of the first and third degree anger and the role of rage in mental competence. Serious disagreements however, were argued among jurists on the role of second degree rage. The levels of rage are:

1. First degree

This is identified as rage that is so severe as to render the individual totally unaware of the meaning of what he is saying or the purpose of his action. This level of rage transforms mental status to the level of insanity, so the same rules will apply. Therefore, there is a consensus that declaring a divorce in this state of mind is invalid.

2. Second degree

This rage constitutes a state of anger that does not affect the individual's mind to any severe degree. He can still be aware of the meaning of his words and recognize the consequences of his actions. However, because of the pressure of his emotions and the intensity of his anger, he may do or decide on things that he does not exactly mean. He is likely to regret what he has said or done the next day. On this issue there are serious disagreements between Islamic jurists. The majority have ruled that since the man was aware of what he was doing or saying, the insanity rule cannot apply and the divorce should pass as valid.

Ibn Qayyim al-Jawziyyah voiced the opinion that if a divorce was declared on the spur of the moment, it should be ruled invalid if anger was at the point of temporarily overwhelming the man's judgment, and if the divorce statement was made as an angry outburst such that the man's intention was impaired by his anger. Note here the choice of emphasis on 'the man's intention' rather than his mind or mental capacity.

Ibn Qayyim al-Jawziyyah was a highly respected jurist of the Ḥanbalī school, even though he was among the minority who supported this view. His ruling is the most popular in the Islamic world today. His decision of invalidating the divorce declaration should only be decided upon by a judge, who will evaluate the degree of the rage and decide accordingly.[7]

3. Third degree

This level of anger does not cause any impairment of judgment or intention. It can occur in any marital argument. The man declaring the divorce may be angry but during the process of pronouncing divorce he is fully aware of his intentions. There is usually not much emotional or affective outburst. If the man wants to change his mind about the divorce decision afterward, his wanting it is insufficient grounds for canceling the passage of the divorce. The divorce will remain valid according to the consensus of all Islamic jurists.[8]

THE *SAFĪH* OR 'FINANCIALLY INCOMPETENT'

A *safīh* (see above, pp.21 and 48) is held to be incompetent to make financial transactions and a guardian is assigned by the court to handle them for him. While the *safīh* is not mentally impaired in the usual sense of the phrase, most schools of jurisprudence withhold certain civil rights, such as following a profession and becoming involved in some contracts, from a *safīh*: the competence to pronounce divorce was included. However, the Ḥanafī school rules against this: it does not normally deprive the *safīh* of any civil rights, including the right to divorce.[9]

UNDOING THE MARRIAGE, OR *KHULᶜ*

Under Islamic law, marital contracts can be terminated by several means – divorce, annulment, and undoing of marriage are a few of them. Annulment means canceling the marriage so that in law everything stands as it was before the marriage. Undoing, on the other hand, is a concept unique to Islamic law. The Arabic term used for it, *khulᶜ* (literally, 'removal') refers to a form of breakage of marriage much like divorce but different from it in several respects, summarized in the following points:

1. Unlike divorce, undoing of marriage is an agreement between the husband and wife. There can be no undoing without mutual agreement. Divorce, on the other hand, is the choice of the husband alone.
2. As a direct result of undoing requiring the consent of the wife, the husband has the full prerogative to break the marriage through divorce if he so wishes; it is presumed that the husband would have no need to consent to the procedure unless it directly benefits him. This usually comes in the form of compensation to the husband. Some schools even define *khulᶜ* as "a form of divorce with compensation to the husband."
3. Unlike divorce, the *khulᶜ* cannot be revoked by the husband. The husband cannot return his wife to the marriage without

her consent. In regular divorce, the husband has the right to take his wife back within the first 100 days of the declaration of divorce, with or without her consent. This period of time allows a pregnancy to become evident, it will also prevent the woman from remarrying before becoming absolutely certain that she is not pregnant. (It is important to note that the husband's choice of calling his wife back into the marriage is removed with the pronouncement of the third divorce.)

4. Unlike divorce, the *khulᶜ* is reversible regardless of the number of times it is carried out but always and only with the consent of the wife. Divorce is irreversible after the third declaration, and the couple cannot remarry unless the wife marries and divorces another man. According to some scholars, this marriage has to be genuine and not arranged to enable the ex-husband and ex-wife to re-unite. The reversibility of *khulᶜ* is also a subject of controversy between the major schools of jurisprudence; the Ḥanbalī school allows it.

COMPETENCE TO UNDO THE MARRIAGE

Whereas only the husband can pronounce divorce, and only his mental competence to do so is an issue, the *khulᶜ* or undoing pro- cedure requires the agreement of both husband and wife, and therefore, mental competence is a requirement for both since *khulᶜ* can entail a form of compensation which may include money, competence for financial dealings is required of the wife. The detail of the arrangements is subject to some differences among the schools of law.

The Ḥanafī school does not allow monetary compensation to take place if the wife is a minor – old enough to understand the meaning of undoing as a process of separation, but not yet financially competent. That does not mean the undoing cannot take place. If a man proposes to his minor wife that they undo the marriage for a certain amount of money given to him, the couple should separate, as in any divorce.

However, because the wife in this case is competent to consent to the undoing as a means of separation but is not competent financially, no financial obligations can be placed upon the wife.

The wife's father cannot undo his minor daughter's marriage unless he gives the compensation from his own money. As a matter of fact, even if the wife is an adult, the father can pay for her undoing if he wishes to, with or without her consent. This rule, however, is debatable among scholars. Those who agree with the validity of a father undoing, regardless of his daughter's consent, explain it on the basis that the undoing was in lieu of a divorce, which is in the hands of the husband anyway. The process was simply a divorce with a compensation given by the father; the husband is in charge of keeping the marriage intact, and in that case may choose to break the marriage by an agreement with his father-in-law which involves an amount of money or other form of compensation.

A mentally healthy adult woman who is declared financially incompetent (*safīh*) cannot undo a marriage. So if this ever happened, it would be a form of divorce and no compensation would be awarded to the husband. Some scholars believe that even if the woman is not formally declared financially incompetent, she does not have the right to consent to undoing if she was known to be reckless with money or an excessive spender. A woman declared *safīh* can, however, consent to undoing if her officially appointed guardian approves it, according to some schools. The Ḥanbalī school, however, disagrees and does not give the right to the guardian to give compensation on behalf of a financially incompetent woman.

As for the husband's competence, there are slightly different rules. In the case of a minor husband (unlike a minor wife where the undoing does take place but the compensation is not awarded) or one who is incompetent to divorce for reasons of insanity or financial incompetence, the undoing process cannot take place. According to the Ḥanafī school, the guardian cannot divorce on behalf of the incompetent. The same rule holds in the case of *khulʿ*.[10]

CHAPTER SIX

Child Custody in Islamic Law

DEFINITIONS

The Arabic equivalent for the term 'child custody' is *ḥaḍānah*, from *ḥuḍn* (literally, the part of the body between the armpits and the knees) which means the bosom or lap where the mother nurses the child. *Ḥaḍānah* can also mean the 'raising of a child' and 'nursery' or 'creche'. Its technical, legal sense is defined in Al-Ṣanᶜānī's *Subul al-Salām* as: "The keeping of the person who cannot be independent, or carry his or her own responsibility, and raising and protecting him or her from what can hurt."[1] It is defined in Al-Kāsānī, *Badā'iᶜ al-Ṣanā'iᶜ* as: "The act of having the mother keep her child by her side and away from the father, so he or she would live with her to raise and keep safe and wash his clothes."[2]

CHILD CUSTODY VS. GUARDIANSHIP

The concept of child custody in Islamic law carries a somewhat different meaning from that in secular law. The latter means full responsibility in the form of legal guardianship which usually also includes immediate care and control; child custody in Islamic law is divided between having a caring responsibility, the responsibility for looking to the immediate needs of the child, and custodial control of the child's affairs generally. In Islamic law, in normal circumstances, the father remains the custodial parent in the latter sense, that is the legal guardian, whether the child is actually living with him or with another person.

Accordingly, in Islamic law, child custody is dealt with in two forms. One is 'residential' or 'care' custody and the other is 'guardianship' custody. The former covers full responsibility for the child's immediate needs, including feeding him, keeping him well, sending him to school, and normal medical care. Sending a child to school in the morning is the responsibility of the residential custodian, while choosing a school is the responsibility of the guardian, that is, the father. The latter includes full responsibility for the child's welfare, including decisions concerning educational and non-emergency medical treatment, and in dealing with the child's money and signing contracts on his behalf, including any marriage contract. If there is a medical emergency, this is the responsibility of the custodian to deal with as would be a minor vaccination or cold. Deciding on non-emergency medication such as an operation or surgery would be the guardian's responsibility. Whereas the guardianship custody is unquestionably given to the father or the next male kin, the mother or the female next in kin has the residential custody.[3] The Islamic jurists disagreed on many issues related to residential custody, but there was no controversy about legal guardianship. In the discussion following, we shall use the term 'custody' to mean ' residential custody', and 'guardianship' for the other kind.

THE MOTHER'S RIGHT TO CUSTODY

The Islamic law bases its decision on giving the right of custody to the mother on more than one source. The first is the Qur'an, the second is the Sunnah, and the third is the consensus of juristic opinion or *ijma*ᶜ.

The Qur'anic Source

The jurists deduce that the mother is the first person to be awarded custody from the verse in the Qur'an, "... the mother should not receive harm by her offspring" (2:233). So the mother should not be harmed by being deprived of custody of her child.[4]

The Sunnah Source

ᶜAbdullah Ibn ᶜUmar reported that a woman once came to the Prophet complaining that her husband had divorced her and demanded that their son be kept by him. She had dramatized her situation with a poetic metaphor, saying that her body had been a vessel for him, her breast had been his drink, and her lap his retainer. The Prophet then said: "It is your right to keep him unless you remarry."[5]

This saying was interpreted to mean that the mother has custodial rights which she can lose if she remarries. The woman's right to custody was also supported by Ibn ʿAbbās's judgment in a custody dispute when he told the father: "Her odor, her bed and her heart is better than yours, till he grows up and chooses for himself."[6] That judgment indicated that the mother should be awarded custody and most Islamic jurists have accepted that.[7]

The Consensus

There is a consensus among Islamic jurists that the custody should be awarded to the mother unless she is unable or unfit for that duty. Ibn Taymiyyah affirmed that in his ruling: "As for the young [child], the mother is more fit for his welfare than the father, because she is more gentle to him, and more knowledgeable about his nutritional needs, carrying him and putting him to sleep. She is also more patient and merciful to him."[8]

CAN THE MOTHER REFUSE CUSTODY?

Whether the mother can refuse to take care of her child and accept him in custody was a subject of mild disagreement. The issue here is whether custody and care is an inherent entitlement of the child, or an entitlement of the mother's? If it is the right of the child to be cared for in the mother's custody, then the mother is obliged to provide that care. But if it is a right that the mother is entitled to then she is free to take or forgo this right. Even within one school there is some disagreement about this. Some of the Ḥanafī jurists, for example, believe that custody is the right of the mother which she can decline if she wishes to. Their view is supported by verse 2:233 mentioned above, and by verse 65:6, both verses referring to the choice the mother has in nursing the baby. However, other jurists like Ibn Abī Laylah and al-Ḥasan ibn Ṣalāh have interpreted the very same verse 2:233 to mean that the mother may be ordered to keep the child in her custody.[9]

The issue is not merely an academic one. In certain circumstances the mother might choose to decline her right of custody in return for release from the marriage. This would be done through the *khulʿ*

procedure (see above, p. 61). But in this case, the woman cannot give up her right to custody in exchange for the undoing of the marriage if the right is not hers to renounce. That is to say, if the custody is the right of the child, then she cannot use this right to bargain for her release from the marriage. Only if custody is assumed to be the right of the mother is her renunciation of this right in the *khulʿ* procedure a valid transaction.[10]

The majority of jurists have come to the conclusion that the mother could be obliged to take custody, if there was no other suitable person, and neither the father nor the child had enough money to hire a person for that purpose. The Ḥanbalī school holds that custody is the right of the mother and the child at the same time, if the child has no other person to take care of him.[11]

PARENTAL RIGHTS FOR CUSTODY

The right of the mother to custody is not itself disputed. The schools of jurisprudence do have minor differences with regard to the next in line for custody if the mother for any reason were disqualified or renounced her right, but these are very minor indeed. An overview of the general concept of the next in line for custody will be more worthwhile than dwelling on the small detail of those differences.

The general principle is that the custodial rights of the mother will go to the next of kin among females on the mother's side, her own mother i.e. the child's maternal grandmother, or the great-grandmother, then the paternal grand- or great-grandmother, then the sister, then the maternal aunt. It is important to note that the maternal half-sister is put ahead of the paternal half-sister, and a maternal aunt is preferred to the paternal half-sister.

If the above list is exhausted then custody could be awarded to the father. If the father is not available or does not meet the necessary criteria, custody will go to his father, then his grand- or great-grandfather, then to the full brother, the half-brother, the full paternal nephew, and so on, following the same line as the order of inheritance.

If none of the above is available for some reason, the next order will be from the maternal line of males relatives, such as the maternal half-brother and the maternal uncle and so on.[12]

GENERAL CRITERIA OF FITNESS FOR CUSTODY

The Islamic law stipulates many conditions, failure to satisfy any one of which will make the person unfit and cause him or her to forfeit the right for custody. These conditions include:

1. *Adulthood*

The age of competence for custody is the age of sexual maturity. There is no dispute among jurists on that issue. So if, for example, a sister is to be awarded custody, she must have reached the age of puberty.[13]

2. *Sanity, or Mental Competence*

There is consensus on this issue as well. Not only has the custodian to be sane, but mentally competent as well. A retarded person or one suffering dementia cannot be awarded custody.[14] The Islamic jurists, however, did not define a standard measure of sanity and mental competence. This is a challenge to be taken up by contemporary jurists.

3. *Adherence to the Religious Codes*

This is a very important condition, not from the point of view of rites or cult, but from that of the general moral ethos in which the child is raised and by which, necessarily, his or her character is influenced. As we shall see, many jurists specified some of the same fitness criteria that are most esteemed by late twentieth-century child psychiatrists and psychologists. The term for non-compliance with the religious and moral codes is *fisq* (sinfulness, vice, depravity). A person proved to have committed *fisq* is not recognized as fit for custody under any school of Islamic law. The reason is to avoid harm to the child. Violation of the religious norms will lead to raising a child who is not on the standard expected of a Muslim, which is tantamount to putting the child in harm's way.

Muslim jurists disagree, however, on the level or degree of non-compliance with the religious and moral norms. Some go to the extreme and deny custody to a person who does not pray five times a day, while more lenient jurists consider whether the particular non-compliance can cause the child harm. Some jurists proposed that theft or adultery constitute a clear instance of *fisq*, requiring removal of the child from the custodial parent because it will have a direct and harmful effect on the child if the parent leaves the child unattended. Some jurists went so far as to consider a mother who neglects her child even for what is considered a religiously good reason as sufficient grounds to deny or remove custody. For example, a mother whose devotions in prayer or fasting or other acts of worship were so intense as to cause her to neglect her child would be considered unfit for custody.[15]

The highly esteemed jurist Ibn Qayyim al-Jawziyyah gave a particularly strong and convincing explanation of this matter. As Islamic law allows the marriage of a Muslim man to a Christian or Jewish woman, and they do not have to convert to Islam in order to remain in the marriage and raise their children, many scholars held the decision to leave a child under the care of a non-Muslim mother to be valid. That being so, Ibn al-Qayyim argues, it is logical to regard non-compliance with the rules and norms of Islam as a state of unfitness for custody only if it caused harm to the child. He went on to affirm that if we expect a full adherence to the religious rules and norms (*ʿadālah*) then it will be extremely difficult to find a proper home for the children of a non-Muslim parent. In sum, it is not feasible to deny people custody of their children just because they are non-Muslim; that would be a practice that was never implemented by the Prophet or by his immediate followers.[16]

We conclude that *fisq* is a valid reason to deny custody, but only when it affects the well-being of the child. A more precise conclusion is that causing harm to the child is the primary motivation behind this controversy since child-neglect stemming from over-involvement in religious rites is also grounds for denying custody. The analogy with contemporary concerns to base custody decisions on 'the best interest of the child' is self-evident.

4. *Safe-keeping* (*amānah*)

Amānah has a wide range of meanings (including 'honesty', 'integrity', 'trustworthiness') derived from the root meaning of 'safe-keeping'. Assuring the child's safety and care, an important function of custody, is what the jurists had in mind when using the term in this context. The custodian is expected to give adequate attention to the child's needs. Many scholars considered leaving a child unattended as a major violation of safe-keeping. Al-Zaylāʿī and Ibn ʿĀbidīn put this in terms of the mother going out of the house several times a day and leaving the child in the company of another child below the age of puberty.[17] Whether the mother leaves the house without the child for a good or a bad reason is not the issue, leaving the child unattended is to risk the welfare of the child. This view has led some judges to decide against granting custody to a working mother. But this is a poor interpretation of the law, because the jurists have based this ruling on the fact that the child is thereby left unattended to the point of affecting his safe-keeping. However, a working mother who does ensure the safety of her child could not be classified as negligent merely because she is working.

5. *Unity of Religion*

There has been long-standing discussion and disagreement between different schools of jurisprudence on the relevance to fitness for custody of unity of religion between child and custodian.

Al-Zaylāʿī stated that a non-Muslim mother has the right to keep her Muslim child in her custody as long as the child is below the 'age of recognition', that is, while the child has no grasp of the meaning of religion. According to al-Zaylāʿī, the mother, even if she is a Christian or a Jew, is more loving to her child than any other woman. Love for the child, he added, is not related to a specific religion. This decision stands as long as the child's understanding of religion is not affected. The child should be raised as Muslim. The mother therefore is expected not to feed her child pork or let him have alcohol just because these are not forbidden in her own religion. If those conditions are not met, the child will be removed from the mother.

The Ḥanafī school, as well as some jurists of the Mālikī school, have adhered to the ruling that unity of religion is not an absolute condition for child custody. Some jurists have argued further that even if a Christian, Jewish or Magian mother gave her child a forbidden food or drink, like alcohol or pork, she should be put under the supervision of trusted observers, but continue to care for the child, in order to serve the child's best interests.[18]

The prominent jurist al-Shāfiʿī held that concurrence of religion is a requirement for granting custody. This opinion is also held by the Ḥanbalī school as well. Their argument is as follows:

1. The child in the custody of a non-Muslim might be brought up as non-Muslim.

2. The custody in question is a form of guardianship. The jurists have a general maxim: "No guardianship of a non-Muslim over a Muslim." This is a somewhat weak point since custody and guardianship can be, and are, legally distinct.[19] The Shāfiʿī and Ḥanbalī schools appear to have viewed 'residential custody' as a sub-type of 'guardianship custody'.

   Ibn Qayyim al-Jawziyyah who, as we have seen, strongly opposed regarding *fisq* as an absolute cause for denying custody, did not support concurrence of religion as a requirement. He pointed out the contradiction in the rule of the jurists who supported violation of religious codes as grounds for denying custody while at the same time disallowing the concurrence of religion as a requirement.[20]

3. The remarriage of the mother: There are differences among the schools on how the mother's re-marrying affects her right to custody which, broadly speaking, is not disputed.

   i) Some have held that her re-marrying is a cause for removal of the mother's custodial right, whether the child is a boy or a girl. This is the view of the Ḥanafī, Shāfiʿī and Mālikī schools, and of some jurists of the Ḥanbalī school.

   ii) Others have ruled that re-marriage has no effect on custody in the absolute sense, whether the child is male or female. This position is held by al-Ḥasan al-Baṣrī and by Ibn Ḥazm.[21] It was based on the fact that Umm Salamah, after her marriage to the Prophet, kept her children from a previous marriage with her. This opinion is seldom accepted by the majority of contemporary jurists.

iii) Another opinion is that if the child is a boy then the custody will be removed from the mother since the biological father has the right, and is more able, to raise his child than another man (i.e. a step-father). If the child is a female, however, custody may remain with the mother. This decision was based on the incident when the Prophet awarded custody of a girl to her male cousin who was married to her maternal aunt. This was not seen as a good analogy to follow because that girl went to the care of her maternal aunt. The reason given is that a girl is better cared for by her own mother. This was reportedly the view of Ibn Ḥanbal, but evidence to the contrary is referred to Ibn Ḥanbal as well.[22]

iv) Some have held that if the mother remarries a relative of the child then she will retain custody. They disagreed on the kind of kinship involved; some held the kinship without restriction, others required a close relative such as a brother, or an uncle, that is a person who theoretically was not eligible to marry the child had he not married her mother. This was the position adopted by the Ḥanbalī school and by Abū Ḥanīfah.

v) The rule of the majority of jurists is to consider remarriage a cause for removal of the child from the mother's custody, unless her new husband is a close relative of the child, such as an uncle. This was based (see above, p.65) upon the Prophet's saying to a divorced mother about her son "It is your right to keep him unless you remarry." The concern here is that a step-father who is not a relative of the child will not be so sympathetic to his needs, and may not be or become sufficiently attached to him to give him the care and love he needs.[23]

vi) Capability to take custody. This means physical capability to meet the needs of the child, in other words the absence of any kind of disability that would impair the child's care. Some jurists have compiled a list of physical disabilities that would disqualify the custodian, but this kind of listing is probably irrelevant now. The primary objective is to secure the best interests of the child; the kind of disability is not important, only how it will affect the welfare of the child. An example to illustrate this point is the decision on blindness. Blindness was judged by some jurists not to be a sufficient disability to disqualify for custody. It would disqualify a mother only if she could not get help in the house to keep the child safe. Whether a particular disability is affecting the child's welfare or not, is a matter that needs expert testimony.[24]

vii) Freedom from contagious diseases. The presence of a contagious disease in the mother will disqualify her from custody. This issue is not controversial, although, now that modern medicine has identified some diseases as having been erroneously listed by the jurists as contagious, their list would need modification.[25]

THE CONCEPT OF PERIOD OF CUSTODY IN ISLAMIC LAW

Custody is limited to responsibility for and care of the immediate needs of the child, whereas guardianship remains the right of the father or the paternal grandfather, etc., as explained above. The term 'custody' in this discussion, we must recall, means 'residential custody' or 'care' which is distinguished from full legal custody or 'guardianship'. The distinction is based on the principle that the child's legal identity derives from and is attached to his father and the father's family line. The mother is seen as a vehicle to carry the child, and is respected and held in high esteem as a parent with appropriate rights as such.

This principle inherently carries the limitation of time when the mother is no longer essential to the child and his care should be transferred to the father or his family. It is an important peculiarity in Islamic law that custody considerations are divided into two stages.

The first stage is to determine the right person to whom to award the 'care' or residential custody. The second stage is to determine the length of that custody.

The four main schools of Islamic law have different opinions on this and sometimes there are differences within the same school. The jurists have estimated the period of custody differently, depending on the sex of the child and other psychological and social factors. We will try to explain these factors to the extent possible, bearing in mind that the reasoning underlying the rulings is not always explicitly stated.

The Ḥanafī School

The period of custody according to this school is seven or nine years for a boy. As for the girl, some say until she reaches menarche, and others say till she can conceivably experience pleasure in sexual intercourse. The age that this can happen varies, but it has been estimated to be around nine years. The girl will stay with her father or his family under male guardianship. If no male guardians are available, the judge will assign a trustworthy female, the mother could be considered in that case. The girl will stay with her father till she gets married; if she was married and is divorced or widowed he cannot force her to stay with him unless she proves to be unruly.

As for the male child, he is expected to stay with his father from the age of seven or nine years until puberty. A father cannot force his mature son to stay with him unless he grows up to be ill-mannered, in which case he can force him to stay in order to be disciplined. The father is not expected to continue to support his son financially after puberty unless he is attending school.

The Mālikī School

The Mālikī school identified the time of residential custody for the boy as lasting until the onset of puberty unless he was retarded or insane. This school has also extended the period for the girl to the time of her marriage.

The Shāfiʿī School

The Shāfiʿī school is very liberal on this issue. It has not specified any period for custody. It is entirely the choice of the child to go to either parent or any other relative of his choice. He can make this decision at any age as long as he can understand the matter. Obviously before that age, the child will be with his mother or the nearest female relative. If the boy decides to stay with his mother, he has to spend the day with his father so that he may be trained and disciplined.

The Ḥanbalī School

The Ḥanbalī school has agreed on the custody period as up to seven years for both boys and girls, after which the boy can stay with his mother if he chooses. This may not be granted if he has chosen the less disciplinarian parent, that is to say, a child's wish will not be granted if it is based on his choosing the more permissive parent who is less likely to discipline him. If the boy chooses the mother he has to spend the day with his father who will teach him a trade and discipline him. By contrast, the daughter must reside with her father from the age of seven years since she needs protection, especially from sexual assault, and the father is thought to be a better person for this responsibility.

THE BEST INTEREST OF THE CHILD IN ISLAMIC LAW

The concept of 'the best interest of the child' is not specified as such in the literature of Islamic jurisprudence. However, reading through the laws one can infer that many jurists, given the conditions they indicated for fitness for custody, held the best interest of the child as the main objective. The first requirement is obviously to ensure that the child is cared for by an adult. The second provides the psychiatrist with authority to decide on the fitness of the custodian, based on his evaluation of mental competence. It follows therefore that certain standards should be identified to ensure mental competence. Those standards should be based on what is best for the child. The requirement that the child and the custodian should be of the same religion was based on avoiding conflict between the way the child is expected to be raised by either parent. The fact that some scholars gave the mother the right to keep her child in spite of not being a Muslim while her child is Muslim by birth, shows the effort made to cater for the interest of the child even at the obvious risk of the child being raised by a non-Muslim. The same tolerance is shown in the way they discussed the issue of adherence to religious rules and norms. Granted that some scholars did not countenance any degree of deviation from strict religious observance, others did put the child's interests and safety above over-indulgence in religious observances.

The most significant contrast between Islamic and secular law is regarding re-marriage of the mother as a factor in her losing custody. This ruling was based on the Prophet's decision: "It is your right to keep him unless you re-marry." When this precedent is taken as the only guide on this matter, the decision to consider re-marriage as grounds for losing custody is not debatable, because it is a divinely inspired ruling. However, the matter was debated and by more than one jurist. They did not view the ruling as absolute, because the Prophet did not present it as an absolute rule. Indeed, he actually ruled on similar matters in a slightly different way. For example, he himself married a woman with children from a previous marriage, and she retained custody. That was argued as a special exemption granted for the Prophet in virtue of his status as God's Messenger; moreover, there is no mention of any claim by the father for custody. At any rate, the issue is not settled; in particular, it is important that even those scholars who say the mother loses custody if she remarries, do not consider it an absolute rule. They base their position on the view that re-marriage is a traumatic event for the child. When the re-marriage is not viewed as potentially harmful to the child (for example, when the new husband is a biological close relative), then the mother may keep custody. The importance of the best interests of the child criterion is obvious in the recognition given to mental and physical competence, as well as the freedom from contagious diseases, of the custodian.

In conclusion, we see that what has governed the thinking about custody issues throughout the history of jurisprudence, has been the best interests of the child. The jurists' view was guided by the Qur'an and the Sunnah of the Prophet, plus their own insight into their community's needs and values. These values are strictly related to the customs and traditions of the Islamic culture of their time.

The considerable diversity in judgment of different schools of Islamic jurisprudence might give us room to accommodate individual circumstances that do not conform to the life-patterns seen by the jurists hundreds of years ago. Modern life-styles challenge contemporary jurists to study further those individual variations in order to achieve more appropriate decisions on child care and custody issues. Many of these new challenges have to do with child adjustment and mental health, as alluded to by most Islamic jurists over the centuries, keeping the best interests of the child as a principal criterion. The field of psychiatry has progressed significantly in modern times and consultation with psychiatrists on these matters is expected.

Shaykh al-Leḥaidān, a well-known and widely respected practising judge in Islamic law, has made the following statement:

> The competent psychiatrist undoubtedly enriches the court judgment, and can help broaden the view of awarding the custody. The psychiatrist however has to be an honest Muslim to testify, a non-Muslim psychiatrist, even when he is honest and competent, is ignorant of the rules of the Islamic way of life and may give an ill advised opinion.[26]

CHAPTER SEVEN

Child Abuse and Child Witness

Abuse, neglect and violence against children by their parents or carers have been recognized in many cultures around the world throughout history. Yet it was not until the 1960s that it received the full attention of lawyers in the secular tradition. In 1946 there was a report of a phenomenon described as inexplicable: children with burn wounds and broken bones were investigated. The author of the report did not suspect that the injuries were inflicted by man. Then in 1962 a paper entitled 'Battered child syndrome' attracted the attention of the medical community as well as the media.[1] This was followed by a series of research papers and legislation in different parts of the United States and Europe dealing directly with the issue.

Secular laws define child abuse as: "A care-giver of a child below 18 years of age causing physical or psychological harm, abusing sexually or neglecting that child in a way that threatens his or her health and safety."[2] In the strict sense therefore, child abuse is not considered as such unless it is caused by the child care-giver, who in most cases will be a parent. Child abuse matters are considered civil cases except when the child is abused by a stranger, when it becomes a matter for the criminal law.[3]

Legislation to deal with child abuse has been introduced over the last thirty years, mainly in Western secular states. However, the concept of a child being harmed by his parents or immediate care-givers had been recognized and addressed by many Islamic jurists long before.

CHILD PROTECTION IN THE QUR'AN AND SUNNAH

Islamic doctrines denounced and rejected many of the habits and customs of the pre-Islamic Arabs. Ibn Qayyim al-Jawziyyah commented on the Qur'anic verse "God gives to whomever He chooses females and to whomever He chooses males" (42:49) – that God mentioned 'females' first in order to remind the pre-Islamic community, who did not welcome the birth of a baby girl, that His favor is present in the birth of females as well as males.[4] The Prophet was quoted by Anas ibn Mālik, as saying that whoever raised or supported two girls till puberty, he would be in the "day hereafter, as close to me as the two fingers in one hand."[5] The caliph ʿUmar ibn al-Khaṭṭāb decreed that if a child's parents could not afford to raise him, he should be supported by the public treasury of the Muslims.[6]

Pre-Islamic Arabs were occasionally prompted by poverty to kill their children, especially girls. Another reason for this was the fear that the girls might, when grown up, bring shame on their families by committing adultery. The Qur'an condemned and forbade this practice: "And when the girl-child buried alive shall be asked for what sin she was slain" (81:8–9). It affirmed the right of the child to inheritance, a right that had been denied in many pre Islamic communities. Orphans being more vulnerable to abuse and deprivation of their rights, the Qur'an particularly emphasizes their need of protection and welfare, and commends for them a generous inheritance, for example: "If at the time of distribution of inheritance, relatives, orphans and the meek should be present, give them from it and speak to them with kindliness" (4:8).

The Prophet's teachings have given the right of identity and belonging to all children, so no man can deny the fatherhood of his children. That was done by the strict rule of assigning the child to the man to whom the mother is married. To deny that requires complicated and difficult procedures. The Prophet set the example of caring for children by recommending that only acceptable and beautiful names should be given to them, by himself playing with his grandchildren, and tolerating their games even when he was in prayer. The caliph ʿUmar once removed one of his governors from office because he was not kind enough to play with his children.

PARENTAL ASSAULT AGAINST CHILDREN IN ISLAMIC JURISPRUDENCE

Assault and battery in Islamic jurisprudence is divided into three main categories:

1. The absolute assault against the person, which is an assault that is intended to and does result in death.
2. Assault against the person that was not intended to and does not result in death – the equivalent of 'assault and battery' or 'grievous bodily harm' in secular law.
3. Assault against the person viewed in a different way, which can correspond to manslaughter in secular law.

There is an abundance of discussion in the literature on assaults against less than the person's life when the assailant is not a family member or a child care-giver. However, when the assailant is a parent or an immediate care-giver, the jurists paid little attention to the matter, especially when the assault resulted in some (bodily) harm but not death.

SCHOOLS FOR AVERTING THE *ḤADD* PUNISHMENTS FROM PARENTS

There is an important general principle in Islamic law, based on the Prophet's instruction to judges: "avert the *ḥadd* punishments where there is room for doubt."[7] Many scholars and jurists considered a crime committed by a parent against a child as inherently carrying a cause of doubt.[8] One of the causes of doubt in Islamic law is manslaughter committed in good faith (that is, without intending to cause death and/or intending to do some good), and if it was done in good faith, then the *ḥadd* (death, in this case) would be averted. The majority of jurists have supported averting the application of a *ḥadd* punishment from a father who kills his child, on the basis that such a deed carries the doubt that it could have been done in good faith in the process of disciplining. Averting the punishment was based on a saying of the Prophet: "Do not conduct the father [to retaliation] for [killing] his son."[9] The Prophet also said to a man: "You and your property belong to your father."[10] That saying led the jurists to assimilate such cases to a general principle called "the right of the whole over the part."[11] That is to say, the father is the origin, or the stem, and the offspring is a branch, i.e. part, of him, and the 'whole' cannot be hurt (punished) because of the 'part'.

The jurists who followed the rule of averting the *ḥadd* punishment from the father who kills his child, have deduced the rule also from a precedent of caliph ʿUmar who did not apply the *ḥadd* in the case of a man who had killed his offspring. The caliph said that he heard the Prophet say that a father should not be executed because he had killed his offspring. That verdict was supported by al-Shāfiʿī and most of the followers of the Ḥanafī school; it is also one of the accepted opinions in the Ḥanbalī school. Al-Ḥasan ibn Ṣāliḥ, a highly respected jurist, concurs with this ruling but does not extend it to include the grandparents. In other words, a man could be executed for killing his grandson.[12]

In the Prophetic sayings just quoted, the parent referred to is the father. The majority of jurists have extended the rule by analogy to include the mother.[13] Ibn Ḥanbal, however, disagreed with this analogy. He argued that a woman could not have the same right as a man in this regard because under Islamic law the mother does not carry the authority of guardianship (*wilāyah*). Therefore, a mother killing her child will be subject to the *ḥadd* punishment as if she had killed a stranger.[14] Some contemporary jurists nevertheless include the mother under the same ruling as the father.[15]

The jurists who rejected the *ḥadd* punishment for the parent who kills his or her child decided by analogy that a parent should not receive the *ḥadd* for physically hurting the child either. Parents accused of child abuse are not expected to be prosecuted for grievous bodily harm in the normal way, since there is no prospect of the Shariʿah punishment being implemented.[16]

Not applying the *ḥadd*, however, does not mean that there are no legal consequences. In lieu of the *ḥadd* the judge will order the defendant or his family or tribe to pay bloodwit (compensation). The parent is thus expected to pay the amount of bloodwit due for the kind or degree of injury or for death.

SCHOLARS AGAINST AVERTING THE *ḤADD* FROM A PARENT

There are two principal lines of argument by scholars who do not support averting the *ḥadd* from parents who assault their children. One considered averting the *ḥadd* punishment only if the act was not premeditated. In other words, if the act was a premeditated murder the parent would be liable to the *ḥadd* as in cases where the murderer was not a parent of the victim. The other line was that parents should receive the Shariʿah punishment in the same way as any other person committing the same offense. The principal proponents of this line were ʿUthman al-Batti, Ibn Nafiʿ, Ibn al-Mandhir, and Ibn Ḥazm.[17]

They based their views on the teaching of the Qur'an and Sunnah. Verse 2:178 in the Qur'an legislates that the punishment for murder is explicitly universal, and includes everybody – man or woman, free or otherwise. The scholars affirmed that the Qur'an stresses the equality of all humans when facing justice, and so they could not conceive of any exemption from a clear Qur'anic command. They also derived support from the Prophet's saying as reported by Ibn Mājah that "all Muslim blood is equal."[18] They argued that the Prophetic saying which relieves the father who has killed a child of the *ḥadd* punishment was conveyed through a single narrator and such a *ḥadīth* canot be used to effect an exemption from a general statement in the Qur'an.[19]

The Mālikī Position

The Mālikī school takes a unique position on this matter. It simply makes the motive for the act the primary decisive factor. If the act was clearly premeditated, the parents will be held fully liable for its consequences.

The scholars who altogether reject excusing the parent of liability to the *ḥadd* are the minority and none of them belong to the four recognized schools. The Mālikī school however, holds that fathers are expected to discipline their children and that physical punishment is part of that discipline. Therefore, if a disciplining led to death, it is clearly not premeditated and harm was not the intention. It is then classed as manslaughter and not murder. Further, the Mālikī teaching requires the circumstances of death to be examined in order to determine whether the act was a killing by mistake i.e. wholly unintentional, or there was an element of neglect, an act that is described in Islamic jurisprudence as quasi-intentional. If proved to be wholly unintentional, bloodwit (*diyyah*) should be awarded to the heirs of the deceased. If the act was judged to be quasi-intentional the amount of *diyyah* will be doubled, or at least increased by a stated percentage (*diyyah mushaddada*, meaning more intensified).[20]

The reasoning underlying this opinion is based on the presence of a doubt (*shubhah*). The doubt here concerns the motive. In Islamic jurisprudence manslaughter with a motive that leaves room for the act to be interpreted as either well-intentioned, or unintentional or quasi-intentional, creates sufficient doubt for the *ḥadd* to be averted. The presumption is that it is inconceivable for a parent to kill a child without a good reason. The Mālikī school put that presumption to the test and demanded a reasonable motive, such as the process of discipline, or other proof that the killing was not premeditated for a criminal motive. The other view, described above, which grants full immunity from the *ḥadd*, evidently assumes that the parent must have had an honorable motive, or that the killing was unintentional. That is in addition to the fact of the Prophetic saying, reported by Ibn Mājah and Ibn Ḥanbal: "No parent is driven to punishment of *ḥadd*, because of his offspring."[21] If that saying is taken as stipulating a general ruling, then it cannot be questioned since such an explicit ruling by the Prophet is accepted as a permanent part of the Shariʿah.

PHYSICAL CHASTISEMENT IN DISCIPLINING

In principle the use of corporal punishment in disciplinary practice in Islam is not objected to. Indeed, the most recent child psychologists' advice does not object to it either. There was a time in the twentieth century when the use of corporal punishment in disciplining children was not condoned, but this is no longer the opinion of experts in child care.[22] The Islamic literature contains several arguments for the use of corporal punishment. One of them is the Prophet's recommendation to chastise children if they refuse to pray by the age of nine years.[23]

The Qur'an (4:34) permits the husband in certain circumstances to use physical chastisement to discipline his wife. However, such chastisement for the purpose of disciplining is only permitted under two conditions. One, that it is a last resort after all other means have failed, and two, the chastisement should not be excessive or painful, i.e. it must not be brutal.

The Islamic jurists disagree on the legal consequences of a well-documented accidental death resulting from such chastisement. If a father accidentally kills his child during corporal punishment, some jurists of the Ḥanafī school would not even oblige him to pay compensation. They see it simply as an accident during the course of parental duty. They argue that the disciplinary practice is consented to by God and by the child implicitly. If any consented act results in damage, the damaged party is not entitled to compensation. In the same way, if a physician causes damage to a patient during a therapeutic procedure, the patient is not entitled to compensation (assuming that there was no negligence). Abū Ḥanīfah himself does not, on this matter, agree with the opinion of the majority of the followers of the school named after him. He insists that a father who accidentally kills his child while disciplining him is liable to pay compensation in the form of *diyyah*. He makes the point that, although the disciplinary act was consented to, that consent could not be extended to the act of killing; he refutes the analogy with the practice of a physician. He argues that the removal of liability for compensation for physicians does not derive from the fact that the act was consented to, but from necessity. If physicians are made liable for damages for accidental errors, they will eventually refuse to practice medicine, so liability is subsumed by the need for the continuation of medical services. Such a necessity does not exist in the case of paternal discipline, because fathers will continue to do their jobs as fathers even if they are liable for damage done to their children.[24]

Islamic law does not recognize an age limit for the child after which a parent who causes the child's death ceases to get the benefit of doubt. That means that a father's (or mother's, according to many jurists) killing an adult child carries no legal consequences other than material compensation. An adult child is considered beyond the need of disciplining, but that does not mean that his father ceases to have the authority to correct him for a grave, sinful or damaging act, such as ruining his father's land, or assaulting his father.[25]

The Islamic jurists have not neglected the possibility that a parent can hurt his child for motives other than discipline. Abū Zahrah, a contemporary jurist, has discussed the circumstances in which a father might be motivated to kill his child – for example, a feud with the child's mother, or in order to avoid paying child support, etc. In that case he argues, the Mālikī school would be the most appropriate school to follow: the parent should be held fully liable as if the crime had been committed against a stranger.[26]

LEGAL IMPLICATIONS OF CHILD ABUSE REPORTING

Secular laws around the world have adopted certain guidelines to protect children from parental abuse, mainly by making it mandatory to report suspected abuse of children brought to a hospital emergency room. Since child abuse by definition is an assault caused by the carer, the assailant in most instances is likely to be a parent. The previous discussion leads us to believe that special attention should be given to the requirement of Islamic laws, before we can adopt fully the Western conventions for reporting child abuse. This issue could be addressed under several headings.

1. *Confidentiality*

Confidentiality is held in high esteem in Islamic law, to the degree that a court order cannot breach it. So, in what circumstances can a physician in the emergency room breach confidentiality and report a possible abuse?

Islamic *fiqh* has a general maxim that can be used to override a legal ruling, namely the acceptance of a lesser harm to avoid a greater one. This principle can be adopted if the danger to the child is judged to be greater than the harm done by breaching confidentiality and reporting the abuse to the authority.

2. *Non-Liability for Failing to Report an Abuse*

Unlike secular laws in some Western countries, the physician cannot be forced or obliged to report the abuse unless he or she feels that the situation is sufficiently serious to warrant that action. While the secular laws would make the physician liable if he fails to report a suspected abuse, this liability would not hold under Islamic law. The reason lies in the limited power of the court to overturn protection of confidentiality. In Islamic law, breaching confidentiality is the physician's privilege and the court has no power to force him to do it. The court in Islamic law does not have the same power to subpoena a witness or documentation as exists in secular law.

3. *Child Protection from a Potentially Abusive Parent*

Reporting an abuse and then attempting to protect the child from further harm is a practice that is condoned by Islamic principle, even if the abuser is thought to be a parent. In the discussion on 'care' or 'residential' custody (see above, pp.64ff.), we clearly saw that the best interests of the child is the primary factor in determining custody. Child neglect was viewed as a serious matter by many scholars, requiring change of custodian. Many jurists have linked the disqualification on grounds of *fisq* (i.e. non-adherence to the Islamic code of ethics and morality) with child neglect. They have argued that *fisq* will lead to child neglect and poor discipline and hence it should be a ground for removing a child from the care of the person involved.[27] Neglecting the child even to satisfy an over-zealous attachment to religious devotions was seen as unacceptable, and custody was removed from the parent who failed to attend to the child's needs for these reasons.[28]

4. *Munchausen's Syndrome and Other Mental Disorders*

The role of mental illness in producing ill-fitted social behavior, such as child abuse, is well covered in the Islamic jurisprudence. Mental competence is a basic element of evaluation for custodial right. Munchausen's syndrome by proxy is probably the leading cause of child abuse in parts of the Arab world, according to published studies on child abuse in Saudi Arabia.[29] On this issue there is no disagreement between the major schools of jurisprudence. The mentally ill parent is unfit to carry out parental duties, and not liable for the consequences of conduct that is the direct result of mental illness.[30] The above rule will hold for all kinds of mental disorder including mental retardation. Whether this rule can cover patients suffering from Munchausen's syndrome by proxy is a subject that will require further study.

5. *Evaluating the Physical Evidence of Abuse*

Signs of physical injury on a child do not of themselves constitute a case of abuse. The Islamic law does allow a measure of physical punishment in disciplining children. The right of the parent to decide the type and severity of physical punishment is well preserved. Therefore, the deciding factor in diagnosis of child abuse has to be based on parental intentions. If the intention was to discipline, the injury in question could not be classified as abuse because Islamic teaching protects the parental right to choose the method of discipline. The Islamic jurists would not prosecute or demand compensation if the child accidentally died in the process. As long as the intention was for the presumed benefit of the child, the assault could not be classified as abuse and the child could not be taken away from his parents unless the physical injury was thought to be caused by intentions other than discipline. This would be the case in abuse caused by some kinds of mental disorder, such as Munchausen's syndrome by proxy, or by jealousy, or by using the child in adult quarrels. (The author of the present work, for example, has treated a severely scalded infant whose injuries were inflicted by his mother in order to keep her husband occupied and away from his second wife.)

One has to remember that the final decision must be based on the best interests of the child. Islamic law gives the judge the right to take the child away from the custodial parent, if the child's interests are violated. So, if a well-meaning parent was unable for some reason to confine his discipline to good corrective practice, removal of the child from that parent's custody should be considered and decided by the judge.

6. *The Criminality of Verified Abuse*

When the abuse is documented and verified, it is not expected to be brought to court as a criminal case, regardless of an intention to assault and the severity of the damage to the child. This conclusion seems to follow in the light of the scholars' view that a parent is not to be made liable for assaulting his child, even if that assault leads to death. However, we may also bear in mind that there are Islamic juristic opinions which do not interpret the Qur'anic verses and the Prophetic sayings in a way that absolutely excuses the parent, in such cases, from liability for the consequences (see above, p. 80).

CHILD WITNESS

Islamic jurisprudence has given a lot of attention to legislating on and regulating the requirements for credibility of witnesses. There are numerous conditions and situations that can affect the credibility of a witness. This is not the place to go into the detail of these conditions, but, since the value of the testimony of a child is linked directly to the issue of credibility, we will address the matter briefly in order to clarify the general perspective.

The question of the child's credibility as a witness frequently arises in child abuse cases. The scope of abuse in such cases goes beyond the assaulting behavior of the parent. Abuse of children can be caused by any relative or non-relative and is likely to involve sexual abuse. Dealing with such abuse, medically or legally, requires, more so than any other form of abuse, the cooperation of the child to describe what happened. Sexual crime in many instances does not leave much material evidence on the child's body.

Conditions or Requirements of a Credible Witness

Islamic jurisprudence indicates several parameters to establish witness credibility. If a person is thought not to meet these requirements, he is declared non-credible and ineligible to testify. Eligibility to testify and credibility can be used interchangeably because they both have the same meaning in Arabic, namely fulfilling "the conditions required for the acceptance of testimony (*shurūṭ qubūl al-shahādah*)." These conditions are outlined under three main headings, on which all the major schools of jurisprudence are unanimous except for very minor details. These conditions are:

1. The witness is a Muslim.
2. The witness has attained puberty.
3. The witness is sane.
4. The witness is mentally competent to recognize the value of the testimony.
5. Fair-mindedness and honesty (*ʿadālah*).

The Shāfiʿī school includes other criteria such as: being a free person (i.e. not a slave), an intact sense of fairness, avoidance of major sins, and no criminal record. The Ḥanbalī school adds the ability to speak, but some accept the testimony of a mute person if he is able to convey what he needs to by non-verbal means. This school also requires good memory and identifies the quality of *ʿadalāh* in the witness by his adherence to the Islamic codes and the obligatory prayer-rites, and that, in accordance with God's orders, he avoids major sins.

One might infer from the above that a child below the age of puberty is not eligible to be a witness. This, however, does not exclude the child from appearing in court. He can be brought to court under two conditions:

1. If his mental age is thought to be equivalent to one who has reached puberty. This argument is based on an interpretation of a Prophetic precedent and builds an analogy on it. Shaykh al-Leḥaidān offered an analogy with the Prophet's appointment of ʿUsāmah ibn Zayd ibn Ḥārithah to lead the army to fight the Romans when he was young and very much older and more senior people were under his command. This opinion is a conclusion yet to be supported by other scholars [31]

2. The child's testimony may be accepted as circumstantial evidence, and not given the full weight of a witness's testimony. This kind of evidence is termed *qarīnah*. *Qarīnah* is any kind of material or other evidence that adds to the knowledge of the court about the case, but does not carry the strength of a witness testimony.

3. The child's testimony or account of what happened could be entertained through the testimony of an expert. Expert testimony is held in high esteem in Islamic jurisprudence, so much so that some jurists are quite satisfied with one expert testimony as against the two witnesses usually required as a minimum to prove a point in court. The expert witness is used when the judge is in need of help to evaluate evidence that falls beyond the scope of his expertise. Islamic jurists have addressed the value of expert testimony in areas such as medicine, engineering and other technical matters. By analogy the psychiatrist's expertise in evaluating child abuse and the credibility of the child testimony in question may be usefully admitted. However, only the judge can rule on the need for an expert witness. Neither the defense nor the prosecution can demand an expert testimony; they can ask for it, and the judge may accede to or refuse such a request.[32]

The Testimony of the Child Against Parent

The child must have attained the age of consent, i.e. puberty. Otherwise, he is not eligible to be a witness at all. There are only very slight differences among Islamic jurists on the acceptance of the testimony of a child against his parent. The child has a vested interest in the welfare of his parents, therefore if his testimony is to their favor it is regarded as questionable. The Ḥanafī, Shāfiʿī and Mālikī schools, and the most popular view within the Ḥanbalī school, have all supported this position. The Shāfiʿī school makes some exemptions, if there was proven animosity between parent and child, then a testimony to the parent's favor may be accepted.[33] Ibn Qayyim al-Jawziyyah, a Ḥanbalī jurist, made the point that if any vested interest in the testimony is not apparent, a child's testimony against the parent can be accepted. This might be the situation if the child is a witness to a marriage contract, a divorce decree, or commercial transaction.[34]

The testimony of a child against his parent is a subject of minor disputes. Al-Qurṭubī stated that there is no disagreement among scholars that the testimony of a child against his parent is acceptable, and does not constitute a sinful action.[35] This position is supported by the

Qur'anic verse which states that "people should be supporters of justice, and witness to God, even if it was against themselves and their parents and relatives ..." (4:135). However, some Shāfiʿī scholars have argued that a child's testimony against a parent should not be accepted in issues related to Shariʿah punishments involving death, lashing or cutting a limb, because parents are immune from that kind of punishment for a crime against their child. In other words, if parents cannot receive the *ḥadd* punishments, when they commit a crime against their children, then the parent should not be liable to get this kind of harm through the witness stand.[36]

CHAPTER EIGHT

Psychiatric Malpractice and Liability

MALPRACTICE

Malpractice is defined in secular law as a tort, committed by a physician or other professional, that leads to damage to a patient or client. A tort is a civil (non-criminal) wrong, based on a breach of contract by one party, that leads to damage to another party, for which compensation is expected and can be demanded in law.

Islamic jurisprudence has long recognized the right of the individual to be compensated for damage caused by others. The Shariʿah has made a clear distinction between forms of civil compensation and punishments for criminal acts. A person may be pronounced not guilty by reason of insanity, but he is still liable for damages and expected to pay compensation. Professionals such as physicians may be protected according to the privilege of their practice, but they can be held liable for damages in certain circumstances, for example, negligence.

DUTY

The patient has to prove that the relationship he has with his physician carries the duty to be treated in a non-negligent way, before he can claim that the physician's neglect has caused him damage. In other words, there must be doctor-patient relationship in the terms explained in Chapter 1 (see above, pp. 4–6). In psychiatric practice the doctor–patient relationship may start in a variety of ways: giving advice to a friend or neighbor, offering interpretations, or prescribing medication during the course of an independent clinical evaluation. Even providing care over the telephone will initiate a duty and consequent liability for negligence if the person involved assumes that he was accepted for treatment.

The duty in Islamic law carries basically the same meaning. As in most secular law, Islamic law does not consider a doctor–patient relationship to have been established through a medical evaluation for the interest of a third party, where no therapeutic services have been rendered. Al-Anṭākī, a well-known eleventh-century physician and Islamic scholar, has made the point that practice of medicine cannot be defined as such without providing some kind of treatment. A routine evaluation therefore is not considered a practice of medicine and would not carry with it the duty and liability.[1]

Islamic law does, on the other hand, impose a duty to care for any person who is in need of that care. In other words, while Anglo-American laws by and large do not oblige the physician to render medical care for anybody he encounters outside the terms of his practice, the Islamic law does impose this kind of duty. According to the Mālikī school, the physician is liable for damages caused by withholding treatment if he refuses to treat the patient, providing there is no other physician around to do it.[2] The Ḥanbalī school takes the same position, but does not approve a specific punishment.[3] The Shāfiʿī school does not share this view, because they hold that liability cannot come about by not doing something, by absence of action.[4] The position of the Ḥanafī school is undecided on this issue.

NEGLIGENCE

Once a physician–patient relationship is established by providing care, the physician is expected not to be negligent. Since the term negligence is a relative one, external standards of care have to be established. With few exceptions, malpractice laws have traditionally held that the customs of the profession are taken to be the standard of care common to all professionals of similar training and theoretical orientation, against which negligence is judged.

In Islamic law, the term negligence is identified by the definition of 'medical responsibility'. Any medical practice that deviates from or violates the terms of responsibility is considered a form of negligence. The term responsibility is frequently used in Arabic in the context of 'liability', and at times the two are used interchangeably. Consequently, it is defined, according to Shaykh Mubārak, as 'the effect' of the physician's causing harm which may lead to a *ḥadd* punishment, or a judicially decreed punishment (*taʿzīr*), or monetary compensation (*ḍamana*).[5] This definition takes account of the actions that make the physician liable, rather than of the medical responsibility of a physician as it was expected to be discharged, which can include care and treatment for the medically ill. Along these lines, the forms of malpractice for which a physician is held liable are the following:

1. Intentional harm.
2. Unintentional harm.
3. Violation of professional standards.
4. Ignorance.
5. Treatment without consent.
6. Deception.
7. Refusal of treatment.
8. Breach of confidentiality.

There is obvious overlap between the different types of malpractice, as classified above. The list includes issues that are considered under quite different headings in secular law. For example, misrepresentation and any other kind of intentionally harmful act could be addressed under one heading. Violation of professional standards is a form of neglect and could be discussed as such. The misuse of pharmacological agents or procedural operations are forms of unintentional acts. We will discuss these matters in the order in which they are presented in the Islamic texts, in order to follow the Islamic legal viewpoint with minimal alteration.

1. INTENTIONAL HARM

An intentional harm done by a physician through whatever means is considered a criminal act. Therefore, it should not be listed as a form of malpractice; however, it is so listed in the Islamic literature. A crime of that nature will be judged like any other criminal act. There is unanimity on this among the schools of Islamic jurisprudence. If the intentional act leads to the death of the patient the death penalty is expected.[6]

Some Islamic jurists have included the act of treating a patient without his consent under the same head as intentional harm, if such treatment resulted in harm to the patient. Al-Nawawī, a widely esteemed Islamic jurist, is credited with the statement that if a physician excised a diseased part of a patient without his consent and thereby caused damage or death, the physician should be penalized by *qiṣāṣ* (measured equal retaliation) which is a penalty applied only for intentional acts.[7] *Qiṣāṣ* can mean a jail sentence, or cutting of a part of the body, or even a life sentence, depending on the severity of the damage inflicted. This view, however, is not shared by the majority of jurists. Some consider that treating a patient without his consent, even if it has indisputably caused harm, is not a form of malpractice provided it was done in good faith.

2. UNINTENTIONAL HARM

The juristic literature covers the issue of unintentional harm caused by medical (including psychiatric) practice in many aspects. As is the case in secular law, the medical error is seen at many levels: an error caused by negligence, an error caused by ignorance, or an error related to neither ignorance nor negligence. Although the classification of these errors is almost identical in both Islamic and secular law, the judicial rulings as to their legal consequences is by no mean the same.

If unintentional harm was caused by an error that is not likely to be made by a professional of similar qualifications, the damage inflicted will be classified as a form of ignorance. In that case the physician will not only be liable for compensatory restitution, but he might be liable to *qiṣāṣ*. Imām al-Shāfiʿī made the following statement on harm caused by a physician's error: "A medical expert should be asked about the nature of that error. If the error was of the kind that can be encountered by a professional and known to happen, and the physician involved admits his mistake, and has sworn that it was an unintentional error, that physician should not be prosecuted. His family, however, has to make the monetary restitution for the damage done and bloodwit if death occured. If the expert testimony is to the effect that no prudent physician could have made such a mistake, the physician involved is to be tried as fully responsible and could receive the *qiṣāṣ* accordingly."[8] The conclusion from that is that for an act of negligence due to ignorance, the physician would be tried as a criminal. If ignorance was not proved, the physician would still be liable for monetary compensation.[9] This judgment was thought to be fair because, in Islamic law, the liability for damages is not affected by the intention. Imām Ibn Qayyim al-Jawziyyah is quoted as saying that "both intentional and non-intentional mistakes are treated equally in regard to the compensation awarded."[10] The question of whether the act was religiously lawful or not, i.e. if the physician sinned by doing as he did, is to be determined by God. The Qur'an has made it clear that God does not punish anyone for an act that was done without malice "And there is no sin for you in mistakes made unintentionally but in what your hearts intend..."(33:5). However, liability for monetary compensation or for punishment of some sort in this life still obtains.

The above ruling is not shared by some scholars of the Ḥanafī school. Al-Ḥaṣkafī, one of the prominent Ḥanafī jurists, declared that the physician is not liable for any compensation as long as he has practiced within the acceptable standards of his profession.[11] Other Ḥanafī jurists have taken a middle position. They ruled for half of the accepted compensation against the physician who caused unintentional damage without being ignorant or negligent, e.g. half the blood-wit in case of death.[12]

The Mālikī school has confirmed the traditional position that any mistake by a physician will make him liable for compensation regardless of the intent, the professional skill, or the standard followed.[13]

The Shāfiʿī school takes the same position as the Mālikī. Some have attributed this rule to the fact that a physician's mistake must have involved an action beyond the implied consent of the patient, for example, damage caused by inappropriate dosage. A consented contract presumably implies using proper dosages of medication.[14] But this example does not reflect the stated rule, because the Shāfiʿī and Mālikī position does not exclude ignorance or negligence. The example quoted reflects an act of ignorance or negligence, or both.

The Ḥanbalī school takes a stand similar to the Mālikī and Shāfiʿī schools in that the physician is liable for monetary compensation for damages, regardless of the standards of practice he followed in what he did.[15]

In every school of Islamic jurisprudence, there are number of jurists who have taken a stand contrary to the ones stated above. Those jurists have ruled that a physician following acceptable professional standards is not liable for any damages and is not expected to pay any compensation as long as there is no evidence of ignorance or neglect.

ʿAbd al-Wahāb, a respected Mālikī judge, has identified the other point of view where the physician is not held liable for damages if he performed his duty in good faith and to sound medical standards. Imām al-Mazrī, another Mālikī scholar, supported judge ʿAbd al-Wahāb in this. Shaykh Ibrāhīm ibn Farḥūn interpreted it differently. He thought that the denial of liability is not only based on the physician's providing care to a sound standard without negligence or ignorance. Rather, there must also have been no error on the physician's part. In other words, Ibn Farḥūn waives liability only in cases where there is no demonstrable error. He makes no distinction in this context between errors of judgment or errors of ignorance.[16] There is an opinion attributed to Imām Mālik himself that "the well recognized physician is not liable for any medical or surgical error, as long as he is known to be a qualified physician."[17]

Imām al-Shāfiʿī stated in his classic work *al-Umm* that if a man was asked to induce a therapeutic bleeding (blood-letting was a common medical procedure at that time), or to circumcise a boy with his consent, or to treat an animal, and he followed the proper standards accepted by the experts of that profession, then he is not liable for the consequences. If, by some chance, he violated those standards, he would be liable even if he was a recognized, qualified professional in that art.[18]

An overwhelming majority of the classical Islamic jurists have affirmed the liability of the physician for a damaging act, regardless of the type of act and the prudence of the physician. The contemporary practice of medicine and psychiatry in the Islamic world has taken the view of the minority and it is not customary to find a physician held liable for damages caused by non-negligent acts. This view was supported by some classical scholars on the basis that if a physician were held liable for ordinary, everyday practice no one would be willing to practice this inherently risky profession.[19]

3. VIOLATION OF PROFESSIONAL STANDARDS

Practicing professional standards of medicine is considered a prerequisite for the waiving of liability for damages resulting from any medical or surgical procedure. That, plus the proper consent, has been accepted by many Islamic jurists as the basis of the legally safe practice of medicine.[20]

Islamic jurisprudence distinguishes professional standards as 'constant' or 'variable'. The constant standards are those areas of medical practice that are not expected to change with time, irrespective of the progress of medical science, and include looking to the best interests of the patient, keeping the terms of the treatment contract with the patient, choosing the safest and simplest means of treatment, and observing the Islamic religious codes during treatment. The variable standards include those acquired skills and knowledge that may be updated as the science progresses. As for those standards of the profession that are universally accepted, or considered to be so, there is no dispute, among either professional physicians or jurists, that violation of any of them makes the physician liable. As for the variable standards, however, there is some room for debate. If the mode of therapy used was unconventional, it is not considered a malpractice unless there is an identified professional view stating that that treatment is harmful. This rule is particularly useful in treating conditions that do not have a universally agreed and accepted method of treatment: many psychiatric disorders fall into this category.

Al-Ṭarābulsī described a particular case in his book *Muʿīn al-Ḥukkām* which is instructive. A little girl had fallen off a roof and suffered injuries such that most physicians decided not to operate on her, except one who was given the consent to operate by the girl's father. The girl died two days after surgery. The judge in the case ruled that the man who operated, even though he went against the opinion of the majority of physicians, was not liable because there was no direct evidence presented to the effect that the chosen procedure was wrong. The opinion of the majority is not by itself sufficient grounds to dispute the method of treatment applied. Since, in that particular case, the medical standards of treatment were ill-defined, they were considered as non-constant standards which permit or require each case to be considered on its own merit.[21]

4. IGNORANCE

Islamic jurists have identified three types of ignorance in medical practice: (1) the physician is an impostor; (2) he is a partially trained practitioner; and (3) he is a recognized, legally practicing physician who gives treatment of which he has no proper knowledge, or has not kept up to date on practices about which he is expected to be knowledgeable.

In the first kind of ignorance, there is no dispute about liability. The second type, however, might call for consideration on a case-by-case basis, since consenting to treatment knowing that the physician is partially trained can affect liability. In the third case, the liability of the physician is undisputed if he was found to be ignorant of a medical matter that he is expected to have known.

Imām al-Ghazālī, a very prominent jurist and scholar, declared that medical practice, especially if it involves any kind of invasive procedure is considered by God a forbidden act and should only be carried out in necessity. Some jurists called for the governor to screen physicians for their knowledge, so that no unqualified person could practice medicine.[22]

A unique situation is created if the patient knowingly consents to be treated by a physician who is not qualified to treat his particular disorder. This happens when a patient has a particular faith in some individual person's wisdom in certain medical matters. When the patient is fully aware of the physician's limited qualifications, yet consents to the treatment, the medical practitioner will not be liable for any damage that might result from his act. This is the stand taken by three out of the four major schools of Islamic jurisprudence. The Ḥanbalī school, on the other hand takes a stricter stand, by denying any untrained or partially trained person the right to practice medicine. It does not recognize the patient's ignorance of the medical prac-titioner's lack of qualification as a basis for denying liability.[23] Ibn Qayyim al-Jawziyyah, one of the most renowned of Ḥanbalī jurists, deviates from the mainstream of his school by making the patient's ignorance of the physician's inadequate qualifications a condition for denying liability and compensation.[24]

Ignorance of the Religious Codes

Observance of the Islamic codes of the permissible and the forbidden, and observance of the ethics of the medical profession, are essential to maintain a religiously sound medical and psychiatric practice. This may include moral values like not hurting a patient by unnecessary treatment with dangerous medications or surgery. It also includes avoiding (when alternatives are available) forbidden substances, like alcohol or pork products, in the composition of pharmacological agents.

The issue here is whether the patient or the physician can be held liable for non-compliance with these codes if either is unaware of the forbidden nature of his act? This rarely becomes a judicial matter as it is normally one left to the judgment of God. However, if somebody felt spiritually unclean because of the use of a forbidden substance in treatment, he might make a claim against the physician on moral grounds. Islamic jurisprudence shares the general maxim that ignorance of the law is no excuse. Imām al-Shāfiʿī pointed out that if ignorance is allowed as an excuse for wrongful acts, then ignorance will become more favored than knowledge, and people would prefer to stay ignorant.[25] That said, there are nevertheless several instances when Islamic figures (like caliph ʿUmar ibn al-Khaṭṭāb), refrained from inflicting punishment on defendants because of their ignorance of the Islamic law. Imām al-Qarāfī said that God has identified some situations where ignorance cannot be an excuse, and He has been forgiving of other matters because of ignorance. From that we conclude that an act considered excusable because of ignorance is one that is judged to be more difficult to identify as wrong, while acts that are easy to pass judgment on are not excused on a plea of ignorance.

5. PATIENT CONSENT

This topic was discussed in some detail in Chapter 3 (see above, pp. 30-34).

6. DECEPTION

There are two ways a physician may treat a patient. The first is when he himself operates on a patient or conducts a medical procedure. In that case the action of the physician is connected directly to its effect on the patient. If the patient suffers harm, intentional or unintentional, the physician is directly involved and responsible. The second method for treatment is indirect, for example when the physician prescribes a medication to be provided by another party, the pharmacist, and then taken by the patient. Here, the physician has treated, indirectly, through a pharmacist.

There are differing views among Islamic jurists on the second method. Some have affirmed that the indirect action should not be seen to have the same legal weight as the direct. That is to say, when the patient himself is administering the prescribed treatment, 'taking the medicine', the liability for a medical error, even an intentional harm, should not be judged in the same way as when the physician is directly involved in administering the treatment. Intentionally causing harm to the patient through indirect means is called by the jurists *ghurūr* or 'deception.' In other words, the harmful outcome of the physician's actions (bodily injury or death) will not be classified as an assault or murder, but as an act of *ghurūr*.

The act of *ghurūr* even if it was intended to bring about the death of the patient is (rather strangely) not classified as a crime according to at least one school of *fiqh*. The Ḥanafī school holds that if a man poisons somebody's drink and the person dies as a result, no punishment should be given to the man; indeed, if he should happen to be an heir of the deceased, he is entitled to his inheritance. The Ḥanafī school argues that the same principle should hold for the physician who prescribes a medicine that leads to the death of his patient because there is time and distance between the act and the event that caused the injury or death.[26]

The Mālikī school has a divided opinion on judging *ghurūr*. The majority view is similar to that of the Ḥanafī school. The minority view is to hold the person committing the *ghurūr* liable for compensation for injury or death.[27] The Shāfiʿī school has no clear written position on *ghurūr* in medical practice. It takes a similar stand to that of the Ḥanafī school on deception in religious counseling. Al-Suyūṭī, a Shāfiʿī scholar, disagreed and declared that a religious counselor should be held liable for deception. The Ḥanbalī school takes a clear position on this issue by making the deceiver in religious counseling or in medical practice responsible for full compensation for injury or death.[28]

7. REFUSAL OF TREATMENT

We noted at the beginning of this chapter that a literal interpretation of the secular law does not impose any duty on the physician, or anybody else for that matter, to treat a patient, even in an emergency, for refusal or neglect of which the physician could be held liable. The Islamic law on the other hand requires the physician to treat a patient in need if there is no other person around to perform that duty. The argument and authority for this rule were set out in some detail in Chapter 1.

8. BREACH OF CONFIDENTIALITY

This subject was discussed in detail in Chapter 1 (see above, pp. 8ff). We would add here that some Islamic jurists have thought that confidentiality should not take priority over public interest.

CONSENTED TERMINATION OF LIFE

In contemporary times, with advanced life-support and life-extending technology, many complex and controversial issues have arisen. Topics like euthanasia, assisted suicide and discontinuation of life-support measures are only very rarely discussed in the contemporary juristic literature in the Islamic world. However, similar problems have been raised by many Islamic jurists in the past, and different and interesting points of views have been argued.

Islamic doctrine forbids the wilful or deliberate termination of a human life for any purpose, no matter how noble. However, one has to make the distinction between an act forbidden by God and an act that is punishable in court. To perform an act that is forbidden by God is a sin on which He will pass judgment. Such a sin may also be defined as a crime and, in a Shariʿah court will be judged and punished as such. Termination of life with the patient's consent may fall under the latter category of forbidden acts.

Many Islamic jurists have argued that although killing is an act of murder as well as a grave sin, death with consent may be a sin that should be left to God to punish, not the court.

Ibn Ḥazm, a renowned Islamic scholar, was one of the few who felt that killing the patient with his consent is an act that should be punishable in law. A branch of the Mālikī school holds the same view as that of Ibn Ḥazm.[29] Most of the Ḥanafī jurists support the notion that killing a patient upon his own request is not a punishable crime, although it should be considered a sin. The same position is taken by some Mālikī jurists.[30] Jurists of the Shāfiʿī school, with a few exceptions, do not stop at withholding the *ḥadd* punishment for that kind of killing. They go further to waive the bloodwit due as compensation.[31] The Mālikī school as a whole adopts the same 'liberal' stance as the Shāfiʿī, making the physician who terminates a patient's life upon his request immune from punishment and, also, not obligated to pay the bloodwit to the relatives of the deceased.[32]

The general stance of the jurists can be explained as a logical inference from the fact that, in Islamic law, in the appropriate circumstances, a killer can be set free. A convicted murderer may not be punished if the victim's family decide to forgive him or to accept bloodwit instead of retaliation. Granted the ruler might decree some additional punishment, this is decided outside the court system. A patient requesting his own death has, in so doing, in effect already forgiven the one who terminates his life for him. It is illogical to assume that the deceased will want a person punished for fulfilling his suicide wish.

This discussion naturally leads to other topics such as euthanasia, assisted suicide, and discontinuation of life support, but these are beyond the scope of this book. Consented termination of a life, on the other hand, falls very much within the arena of forensic psychiatry, since evaluation of mental competence to consent for termination of life is a major psychiatric undertaking. We believe that contemporary Islamic jurists will need to cooperate with psychiatrists in order to identify criteria or tests for competence to consent to have one's life terminated.

DIYYAH: THE BLOODWIT FOR AN ORGAN OR A LIFE

The subject of *diyyah* is of integral importance in applying the Islamic law in the field of medical and psychiatric malpractice. Guidelines need to be evolved, using *qiyās* (analogy), to estimate the amount of compensation to be awarded for damage caused by proven negligence.

Diyyah is a concept particular to Islamic law whereby a monetary value is set for the life of a human being as a whole, as well as for each bodily organ. This concept dates back to pre-Islamic Arabia and the Shariʿah affirmed its validity as a means to keep peace among people and tribes. Thus, if a person kills another, the victim's family or tribe might accept bloodwit instead of having the killer executed. This served as peaceful means to resolve conflicts between tribes and avert clan feuds. It is of particular value in unintentional assaults and accidental manslaughter.

In the case of an intentional act of murder, the Shariʿah gives the right to the victim's heir to decide if he wants to have the murderer executed for the crime or if he will accept the *diyyah*, or forgive the crime outright. If the death resulted from an unintentional act, the heir of the victim has no right to demand execution but may choose between accepting compensation or outright forgiveness. The same principle is applied to injuries. If an intentional act results in damage to an eye, an ear, a nose or a hand, etc., the victim has the right to choose between having the same damage inflicted on the assailant or compensation. If the damage was caused by an unintentional act the victim has to accept compensation. The term for compensation is *diyyah*, but it is sometimes also referred to as *arsh*.

The compensation for an organ is determined by a simple rule which states that any organ in the body is worth the same amount as the whole body if that organ is not paired, like eyes, ears, hands. Therefore a nose has the same value as the whole body in monetary compensation as does a tongue or a penis. A paired organ is worth half the whole body value. If more than one organ serving the same purpose is damaged, like fingers, the whole body value (with minor exceptions) is divided by the number of those organs.

If damage does not involve a whole organ or when the amount of loss of function is difficult to evaluate, a special process called *ḥukūmah* is undertaken. The Islamic jurists agreed by consensus on a particular calculation to evaluate in monetary terms the 'market value' of a human being. The only analogy was the market value of a slave. Assuming the person had been a slave in full health, how much would he be worth after the damage or disability? If for example, a slave had been worth 100 units and this was reduced to 90 units due to the injury, he had therefore lost about 10% of his total market value. The amount of compensation would then be worked out at 10% of the total *diyyah*. This calculation was applied to work out the percentage of loss of function which, when applied to the amount of the full *diyyah*, yielded a precise figure.

The amount of the *diyyah* was ruled by the Prophet himself, and like all divinely inspired rules, is not normally subject to alteration. The *diyyah* for a life is 100 camels. In Saudi Arabia at the present time, that is estimated to be around $4,500. The *diyyah* for any organ that the body has only one of, such as a mouth or a nose, would be the same as for a life, for a paired organ, such as one eye or ear or leg, it would be half of that. If more than one organ is damaged, the compensation is accumulated for each organ so that multiple organ damage may amount to several times more than the full *diyyah* for a life. For example, caliph ʿUmar ibn al-Khaṭṭāb ruled that a man who was battered and lost his hearing, vision, sexual function and cognitive abilities, be awarded 400% of the *diyyah*. Had he died before he recovered from his wounds, his family would have been awarded 100% of the *diyyah* only.

PROBLEMATIC ISSUES ON *DIYYAH* FACING CONTEMPORARY JURISTS

To apply the concept of *diyyah* in contemporary handling of malpractice issues and consequent compensation, presents more than one problem. Some of these issues are unique to psychiatric practice, others are of a more general medical nature. They may include the differentiation between loss of organ and loss of function, the estimation of mental function and grade of impairment, and the value of a particular organ or function to a particular person.

1. In current juristic literature there is no clear differentiation between the loss of an organ and the loss of function. It would seem that the loss of function is reckoned as equivalent to the loss of organ. The loss of hearing, for example, will be awarded the full *diyyah*, while the loss of both ears with the hearing intact will also be awarded the full *diyyah*. By that token, losing both the sense of smell as well as the nose itself might be reckoned at twice the full *diyyah*. This issue is not clearly addressed in the texts of Islamic jurisprudence and needs clarification.

2. This topic is of vital importance to psychiatric practice, especially in workplace injury compensation cases, and disability evaluations. The brain is a multi-function organ. An injury to the brain and other intracranial structures can lead to loss of sight alongside preservation of the eyes, or it can lead to multiple loss of function like memory, cognitive function, emotional stability and so on. Damage to sensory or motor areas in the brain would mimic complete loss of function of a limb or limbs. A single limb is equal to half the full *diyyah*, so it seems logical that the brain should be dealt with as a multi-function organ and the amount of *diyyah* awarded should depend on how many functions were lost and to what degree.

3. There is no clear differentiation between the value in general of *diyyah* for an organ or for a life, and the particular value

of that organ to a particular person or family. Can we reckon the loss of a hand to a surgeon as having the same value as the loss of a hand to a psychiatrist? A psychiatrist can still earn a living with only one hand but a surgeon cannot operate without both hands. The same question arises for full *diyyah* in case of death: the compensation as it stands now in Islamic law is fixed, regardless of the kind of work or level of income the deceased person was making or the economic consequences of the loss to his family.

4. The process of *ḥukūmah*, calculating the amount of damage by estimating the 'market value' of the injured person if he were to be sold as a slave is surely impossible to apply in this age. Slavery does not exist anywhere in the world and we cannot know how to estimate the value of slaves. Nevertheless, the process might be adapted through analogy: the aim would be to estimate the percentage of damage and its value to that particular individual, taking into account the economic loss caused by the injury or death. This would allow calculation of the value of loss of function in direct relationship to the particular value of that function to the particular individual. In this way the question raised in the previous paragraph might be resolved – provided such an adaptive analogy were acceptable.

AFTERWORD

I have already set out (in the Introduction) some of the circumstances in which this work was conceived. It is very much in the nature of a preliminary survey of some of the issues facing the practice of forensic psychiatry in Islamic contexts. It would certainly be premature to draw any major or definite conclusions. Nevertheless, I permit myself to reflect here in general terms on a number of important points.

First of all, it must be conceded that the concept of forensic psychiatry, whether as an academic discipline or as a practical science, has only very recently been introduced to the legal system in the Middle East. In fact even today, the subject does not receive special attention in medical school curricula. It became evident to me over the decade and a half that I have served as a chairman of the Scientific Committee on Mental Health (the main consulting body in psychiatry to the Ministry of Health in Saudi Arabia) that the management of legal issues in the mental health field is a sensitive subject from which officialdom turns away as much as it can: efforts to formulate a Mental Health Act have faced innumerable unexplained delays, with many proposals and recommendations remaining unanswered for years. Regulations suggested by other committees and concerned individuals have suffered the same fate. To date, not a single proposal (the first was put forward fifteen years ago) has been formally approved. It seemed to me that one of the reasons for this had to be the lack of knowledge and understanding about what forensic psychiatry is and how it relates to the Shariʿah. Another factor inhibiting the decision-making processes was certainly the perception that forensic psychiatry, taught through medical and psychiatric texts written almost exclusively by Western authors, must be alien to, or in conflict with, fundamental Islamic legal concepts. As explained earlier, I discussed the idea of presenting the subject of forensic psychiatry in

Arabic and in the light of Shariʿah concepts with a prominent judge in the Ministry of Justice, Shaykh Ṣāliḥ al-Leḥaidān. Al-Leḥaidān welcomed and encouraged the idea which was realized as a book some years later. That book, *Al-Qaḍā' wa Niẓām al-Ithbāt fī al-Fiqh al-Islāmī wa al-Anẓimah al-Waḍʿiyyah* (1996) opened the way to discussion of many points of difference and conflict between the Western and Shariʿah legal concepts in this field. The present work continues and enlarges that discussion.

What emerges clearly from this study is that, while the concept of forensic psychiatry as such is not to be found in traditional Islamic literature, the major issues of concern in the field were discussed with considerable sophistication and precision by the Islamic legal scholars of the past, albeit under diverse heads. For example: mental competence and its social and legal consequences in different areas of life, medical negligence and malpractice and degrees of liability, issues related to child care and custody, the complexities of establishing individual intent, the importance of doctor-patient confidentiality and the powers of the court to breach such confidentiality – these and other subjects were presented from various viewpoints from within the Islamic legal tradition. It is gratifying to observe, alongside the sophistication of the Islamic scholars' discussion of such matters, their humanity and compassion, their commitment to fairness and reasonableness, their tolerance of diverse opinions, and their flexibility – their readiness to address concrete situations in the light of enduring general ethical and legal principles.

Thus, we hope to have demonstrated that the Islamic perspective on some of these issues can illuminate the thinking and practice of modern 'secular' forensic psychiatry. Equally, on the Western side, there have been major advances, in medical-technical knowledge and expertise, as also in legal concepts, which the Islamic legal system could usefully take account of and, within the bounds of permissible ijtihad, adapt to suit its own traditions and ethos. In short, there is a potential for mutual benefit in studying the two traditions, as it were, side by side.

To be sure, it is almost never a straightforward question of preferring this tradition or the other, or of simply adding a particular practice in one tradition onto the practices of the other. Each tradition constitutes a whole and has evolved within its distinct religious and cultural milieu. Learning and adaptation must therefore be patient, subtle and cautious. An example is the difficulty of balancing doctor-patient confidentiality and the court's need or right to breach that confidentiality in certain circumstances. As we saw, in the Islamic legal system the concept of a subpoena is not well outlined and stands in need of clarification, even though obliging a witness to testify is not absolutely unknown in Islamic jurisprudence. In contrast to the subpoena powers of a secular court, confidentiality is held by many Islamic jurists to be so sacrosanct that a judge can almost never force the doctor to betray the patient's trust. The Shariʿah's stand on confidentiality causes us to reflect on the 'Tarasoff rule' whereby a physician who learns from his patient of a threat to a third party is obliged by law to disclose that threat to the potential victim and/or the police. A practical consequence of this rule has been that many patients do not make full disclosure to their therapist so that the therapist neither gets to know of any threat to a third party nor is able to try to dissuade the patient from carrying out the threat. The Tarasoff rule, in the opinion of many, has considerably disrupted patient-doctor trust.

Another point of significant divergence between the two traditions is the issue, in criminal cases, of the level of intent and premeditation. There is no reason to believe that Islamic jurists may consider reviewing and refining the level of cognitive intent in criminal actions beyond the *ʿamd* and *shibh al-ʿamd* concepts. Similarly, the definitions of insanity found in *fiqh* literature do not match the level of sophistication reached in modern psychiatry. New rulings should be envisaged that go beyond the 'McNaughton rule'. That rule might be too stringent in certain cases; other insanity tests determined by the American Law Institute and the American Congress are also unlikely to be appropriate for Islamic contexts. More suitable rulings, that is, rulings that will directly benefit Muslim communities, need to be worked out. While some distinction is made in contemporary Islamic courts between 'competency to stand trial' and 'insanity', the former is not, as we have illustrated, a matter that has ever been directly or formally addressed by Islamic jurists. It is my view that competency to stand trial needs to be studied, and a ruling that specifies criteria for such competency should be defined.

In most of the secular legal systems in the Western world, the basis for involuntary admission of a mentally ill individual is the level of danger his behavior presents to himself or others, rather than his need for care and treatment when he is mentally incompetent to request or agree to such treatment. That has resulted in leaving hundreds of mentally ill individuals homeless on the street, many of whom then end up, through committing petty crimes, in the prison rather than the mental health care system. As we demonstrated, Islamic law places the burden of responsibility on the society to care for the mentally ill individual, not because he is a danger to himself or others, but simply because he needs care and treatment. Greater weight is given in the modern Western tradition to the state's duty to protect individual liberty than to its duty to care for the individual.

Islamic jurisprudence recognizes many types of mental competence. We have shown that there are concepts and types of competencies that are unique to Islamic law. The competence to undo a marriage; financial competence, maturity or adulthood, and competence of performance, are among examples of legal notions specific to the Islamic tradition. The standards for determining competence to marry and divorce have been particularly well outlined in the *fiqh* literature, unlike other types of competence, where no specific criteria have been spelled out. We argued in this book, that in a number of areas – among others, competence to enter into a contract, to make a will, to stand trial, to consent to treatment – criteria need to be better specified in order to guide psychiatrists when evaluating competence.

The role of psychiatry in legal cases involving family law was raised, to the best of my knowledge, for the first time in this book. We have seen that Islamic *fiqh* is, in the interests of compassion and humanity, flexible and accommodating: a wide variety of Islamic juristic opinions, through centuries of ijtihad, evolved an important principle in child custody, namely the 'best interest of the child.' Child custody is now determined in most cases without the involvement of a psychiatrist. It is our view that an experienced child psychiatrist can provide valuable information that can guide a family court to determine custody on considerations beyond the qualities of the parents involved, by looking directly at the child and deciding on his or her best interest. We also argued in the text that psychiatric expertise is relevant and could be helpful in deciding cases of divorces and undoing of marriages. Such expertise is certainly needed to determine whether a pronouncement of divorce was valid or not: many a family could be saved from an invalid pronouncement, especially as such a pronouncement, when legally accepted, is practically irreversible.

We noted a variety of rulings from different jurists in cases related to medical malpractice. The Islamic legal criteria for deciding medical negligence, ignorance, and violations of accepted professional standards, were discussed in some detail. The discussion of patient consent illustrated the diverse and sometimes contradictory opinions of Islamic jurists. More recent discussions of the concept of consent have broadened to include requests for so-called 'assisted suicide' and 'euthanasia.'

I have, in several places in this book, as well as in the Appendix of case vignettes, indicated directions for ongoing reflection and research. It is my hope that the survey here presented of issues in forensic psychiatry from an Islamic perspective will contribute to further scholarly study of the legal and philosophical arguments, in the light of the Islamic tradition and of contemporary needs, experiences and concerns.

APPENDIX

CASE EXAMPLES

Questions and Answers with Shaykh Ṣāliḥ ibn Saᶜd al-Leḥaidān

TABLE OF CONTENTS

Questions and Answers with Shaykh Ṣāliḥ ibn Saʿd al-Leḥaidān

The examples are, for the obvious reasons, fictional, though details of most are derived from real cases in an Islamic country. They have been designed to give concrete, practical form to some of the matters discussed in the main part of this book. They illustrate some of the more frequently encountered problems in clinical practice, as well as issues that are much debated in the international literature.

The case situations and the questions following them were put to Shaykh Ṣāliḥ ibn Saʿd al-Leḥaidān, a senior practicing judge in Saudi Arabia and consultant to its Ministry of Justice. His reflections and comments are summarized in the Answer section that follows the Question section. The Comment section with which each case ends presents further reflections of the author on the Answer.

CASE I
Confidentiality and duty to protect a third party

A twenty-five-year-old male patient has admitted to his psychiatrist that he is very angry about what he believes to be an unfair judgment passed on his father. He believes that his father has been unjustly imprisoned, as a result of a false accusation made against him by a well-known public figure. The patient actually stated the name of that public figure. He also admits to his own vengeful intentions, and has said that he means to kill the man responsible for his father's plight. The psychiatrist has been unable to persuade the patient to change his mind and he is convinced that the patient will act on what he believes.

Question
Should the psychiatrist inform the police and the person being threatened? Does the action of informing the police constitute a breach of confidentiality for which the psychiatrist is liable?

Answer
Whether the psychiatrist will choose to inform the police or not depends on whether he thinks (a) that the system of government that exists is a just one; and (b) the police are able to properly understand the psychiatric or psychological condition of the patient.

In any case, after he has reflected on those two matters, it is a decision left to the psychiatrist's judgment. Depending on his conviction about, and understanding of the patient's mental state, he may choose to inform the police, with a good account of the patient's state of mind and delusion.

Comment
This case demonstrates the Islamic legal view on what is known in the secular law as the Tarasoff rule. This rule, upheld in almost all states in the USA, is a controversial one. If a patient threatens a third party, the therapist is ruled to have a duty to protect that party, by informing him or her about the patient's intentions. The rule is controversial because it compromises doctor–patient privilege.

CASE 2
Confidentiality vis-à-vis subpoena

A psychiatrist in an Arab country had a patient who admitted to him that he had killed his wife after discovering her affair with another man. He hid the murder weapon in a certain place which he also disclosed to the psychiatrist. The man had been able to remove all traces of evidence against him. During investigation it became known that he was seeing a psychiatrist. The prosecuting attorney wanted the psychiatrist to testify in order to elaborate on the patient's state of mind. The psychiatrist refused to go to court and disobeyed the court subpoena.

Question
Under Islamic law can the judge oblige the psychiatrist to testify, and can he penalize him for not testifying.?

Answer
God has stated in the Qur'an "... let no harm be done to scribe or

witness ..." (2:282).Therefore, neither of these two may be forced, the scribe to write something or the witness to testify.

Comment
This case demonstrates that in Islamic law the power of a court subpoena is not well defined. Whether or not to oblige a witness to testify is subject to the discretion of the judge. In this case, Shaykh al-Leḥaidān ruled that a witness cannot be forced, nor if he refuses to testify, can he be penalized.

CASE 3
Confidentiality of documents vis-à-vis subpoena

A psychiatrist has treated a patient who was a major figure in the political opposition in an Arab country. The man was hunted by the country's bureau of investigation and intelligence service, and subsequently arrested. The psychiatrist was asked to hand over his patient's records and psychological testing material to the investigative body in order to assist them in their interrogation. When the psychiatrist refused, the investigative body got a subpoena from the court, ordering the psychiatrist to hand over the records, and/or to come as a witness.

Question
Does the judge have the right to force the psychiatrist to testify or hand over documents and patient records? If the judge thinks that the best interest of the public will be served by having the documents delivered, can the psychiatrist be forced to release them?

Answer
It would be all right, if there is a just cause and a public interest is served by getting this information, and provided it will not hurt the patient.

Comment
This is another example of the concept of subpoena in Islamic law. The subpoena is ordered to the records and not necessarily to the psychiatrist himself. This might in some people's minds exclude the condition of not harming a witness, since the subpoena is not directed

at a person, but merely at a document or body of documents. The introduction of public interest gives the matter another dimension. The answer differs slightly from the previous one. Here, the psychiatrist can be forced to hand over the records if the patient would not be harmed by it and there is a public interest.

CASE 4
Confidentiality vis-à-vis subpoena or court order

A psychiatrist was treating a patient for mild depression. During sessions the patient told his doctor about a compulsion to have anal sex with his wife, which was done without her consent. The patient then stopped seeing that psychiatrist. The wife filed for divorce on the ground that her husband demanded that kind of sex from her. This sexual practice is a legitimate ground for divorce in an Islamic court. Her husband denied the charges in court. The wife wanted to have the psychiatrist put under subpoena to testify to that fact. The psychiatrist refused, in order to protect confidentiality.

Question
Can the judge call the psychiatrist and subpoena him to testify particularly in light of the fact that, as the husband is forcing his wife to a form of sex that is forbidden, she has the wife's right to have the divorce?

Answer
That no body should be forced to testify is a general rule. Also in the interest of protecting privacy and confidentiality. The wife may insist on divorce or seek an undoing of the marriage (*khulᶜ*).

Comment
This is another example of the confidentiality of the privileged information being given priority in the legal order of things. Some sexual practices are considered forbidden in Islamic law, and thus can be a ground for divorce. However, the wife cannot obtain a divorce unless she can prove harm. In this instance, the judge suggested another way out for her, namely to seek a *khulᶜ* (see p.60 above).

CASE 5

Involuntary treatment of a mentally ill person not immediately 'dangerous' to himself or others

A twenty-five-year-old, diagnosed with schizophrenia (a mental disorder that can lead to insanity), is in a confused, dazed state, rarely leaving the house, unable to care for his wife and children but mostly able to take care of his own immediate personal needs. He responded very well to treatment in the past, to the extent that he became a responsible person, able to support his family. He only regressed or relapsed when he thought he was so well that he did not need treatment any more. This patient is unable to recognize that he is ill and in need of treatment because of his mental illness. Though sometimes unable to take care of himself, he is not a danger to himself or others.

Question

Can a member of his family give consent to have him treated in a hospital against his will? Does any member of his family have more right to give such consent than any other?

Answer

As I understand it, I do not see that he should be put in a hospital. However, if that were necessary, the one responsible for giving consent for his admission would be the next sane adult relative according to the line of inheritance. If the condition was serious, and there was a fear for the patient's welfare (for example, by his neglecting his personal health) or a fear of his hurting other people – God has stated in the Qur'an: "... and do not be thrown by your own hands towards ruin ..." (2:195). That command applies to the patient; it also applies to the patient's clan. So the clan should look after its member, who is mentally ill.

Comment

The answer clarifies the Islamic position on involuntary treatment of the mentally ill. His being a danger or not, to himself or others, is not the decisive consideration as regards committing the patient for treatment. The need for treatment is a duty. It is also the duty of the family or the whole clan or tribe, if necessary. The Shaykh apparently did not see the need for hospitalization in this case, probably because he thought the condition might be treatable on an out-patient basis. However, he did make it clear that patient's needs of treatment are enough reason to commit him, in order to avert deterioration due to lack of care.

CASE 6
A mentally ill person acting from delusion as well as from reality-driven motives

A thirty-year-old schizophrenic was put in a mental institution for treatment of a recent regression in his condition in which he suffered intense hallucinations and delusions. He had started to believe that he was a holy one who was charged with rescuing humanity from evil people. He chased those evil ones in public places, particularly banks. He focused on banks because he was convinced that people attending such evil places that function on the basis of usury must be evil. He was committed to the mental institution before he could carry out any assault. He decided to run away. He climbed a fence at night, knowing that he could be stopped by the security men if he tried to leave by the gate. However, as he went over the fence, he was seen by a guard who fought with him. In order to avoid being detected the man actually killed the guard. He got away, only to be caught by the police shortly afterwards. He denied the fact that he had killed the guard and made up stories to evade the facts. He was put back in the hospital.

What is important here is that man is known to be schizophrenic, and that his delusions about having to attack people who do business in banks are related directly to his illness. Had he killed someone identified within his delusion as an evil one, his crime would have been directly attributable to his mental disorder. But he killed the guard for a reason not connected to his delusions. He also knew that his action was legally wrong and he actually denied what he had done.

Question

Is the man to be held not responsible for his crime because he is mentally ill and ruled as insane? Or should he be held responsible because, in spite of his mental illness, he was aware that killing the guard was a crime punishable by law. He also knew that the guard was not among the evil people his delusions impelled him to pursue.

Answer

Schizophrenia, as I understand it, is of different kinds. It was not clear which one this was. To my knowledge there are at least two general classes, the inherited and the acquired. If the kind this patient is suffering from is inherited, my judgement is that the sentence should be minimized.

If his illness is acquired, as caused by bad upbringing, poor parenting, abuse, or if it came from some reading matter – whoever had a share in causing this condition should share in the punishment.

The patient's ruling should be reviewed regularly, i.e. to identify what type of schizophrenia it might appear to be.

Comment

Reviewing the existing Islamic literature on the role of insanity, there is no formal or explicit distinction between the existence of insanity (*junūn*) in and of itself, and its direct relationship with the act committed. The fact that the accused involved in the crime is insane did not affect the judgment that, being responsible, he should be sentenced for the particular act. So we can safely infer that the mere existence of mental illness does not automatically exempt a patient from criminal responsibility. The Shaykh's answer also raises another issue, namely the concept of partial responsibility. This concept does not exist at this time in the laws of the United States.

CASE 7

A mentally ill person acting out of delusion, aware of the legal but not the moral wrongfulness of an act

A thirty-year-old widow suffering from a severe form of psychotic depression, which can lead to a state of complete or partial insanity, was experiencing strong hallucinations and delusions in which angels called her to come to heaven to meet God. She had to kill herself in order to achieve that goal. She did not perceive killing herself to be an act forbidden by God, believing herself to be a special case since angels were calling and commanding her. She had a five-year-old daughter. Because she was worried about having to leave her daughter without a mother to take care of her, she decided she had to kill her daughter too. She went ahead and did so before cutting her own wrist arteries. Neighbors discovered the mother in time to take her to the hospital where she recovered. The little girl is dead; her mother faces the court. The woman was intelligent enough to know that killing her daughter was a criminal act punishable by law; that had not bothered her because she was counting on dying by suicide anyway.

Question

Do this woman's hallucinations and delusions render her not guilty? Or, since she was aware of the criminality of killing her daughter, should she be held accountable? What is the relevance of her own feeling of innocence in that, as she apparently believed, her action was accepted by God since it was done at the bidding of angels?

Answer

If the diagnosis of her illness is confirmed and established at a high level of scientific expertise and integrity, then the woman should not be tried, because she was motivated by her compulsions, her overwhelming thoughts. Mostly those people who suffer from strong hallucinations are aware of their immediate surrounding and of what they are saying or doing. Partial insanity must sometimes be subject to the same rule as insanity. This patient will not be held liable for her action, or the sentence will be reduced if the insanity state was clearly partial, depending on the detail of the case.

Comment

This case illustrates that knowledge of an act being wrong is not limited to the legal concept of it being wrong (criminal). That is, knowing that the act was wrong and knowing the legal consequences of it are not by themselves sufficient to render a mentally ill person responsible for the crime committed. This woman knew the act of killing her child to be legally wrong, but did not perceive her action as morally wrong. In her mind, what she did was morally right because she herself 'had to' die and she did not want her daughter to be left uncared for after her death. However, such ignorance of the moral wrongfulness of an act must be coupled with mental illness in order to be a ground for acquittal. Most of those who are politically motivated to commit crimes of terror may believe that their action is morally right, but they are nevertheless fully accountable for their actions as long as they are not suffering from a mental illness.

CASE 8

Criminal responsibility of a mentally ill person acting out of delusion but aware of the criminality of his act

Zayd is a twenty-four-year-old man, diagnosed as schizophrenic four years ago and under almost continuous treatment since then. Schizophrenia is a disorder that can be associated with insanity. He suffered from delusions in which he became convinced that his parents were evil and his mortal enemies. He was under treatment in Egypt when he made a decision to kill his parents who were, at that time, living in Kuwait. He planned to go to Kuwait under an assumed name on a false passport so that no-one would suspect that he had left Egypt. He had worked out that, as there would be no evidence in his original passport documenting his departure, he would have a perfect alibi. He then did go to Kuwait as he planned and ended up killing his parents there. However, he was arrested shortly after the crime, before he could return to Egypt.

During the trial the prosecution argued that his mental illness could not be a reason to acquit Zayd by reason of insanity because, in spite of his mental illness, he was well able to recognize that what he was doing was wrong, and because he had premeditated and planned the crime with the aim of avoiding detection. Zayd's defense lawyer argued from medical reports and expert testimony that Zayd was severely mentally ill and that his criminal behavior was prompted by his delusions.

Question

Which of the two arguments is more likely to be accepted? Is Zayd guilty because of his full awareness of the legal wrongfulness of his act? Or is he not guilty because the insanity rule is applicable in his case?

Answer

In this question as in some previous questions the statement that "Schizophrenia is a disorder that might lead to state of insanity" is somewhat confusing and makes me hesitate to answer those questions. As far as I know, schizophrenia is of four kinds. To give the appropriate ruling, the kinds of schizophrenia and their consequences need to be carefully identified. Generalities put someone in my position in need of a lot of time to discuss the case thoroughly.

Should the accused in question be allowed the insanity defense? You have clarified that he was aware of what he was doing, and of the kind of action it was. As I see it, schizophrenia is different in different people according to how severe the delusions are, the sensitivity of the individual, and the nature of the compulsive actions associated with it. It is of two classes; inherited and acquired. The former is most serious because, unlike the latter, all the known characteristics of the state are there. If the accused has the inherited type, then he might get the insanity defense and should get a lighter sentence.

If he is suffering from the other form of schizophrenia, then he should be sentenced like any other person.

Comment

This example was derived from a real case presented in a California court. The accused was found guilty in spite of documented mental illness and the fact that his action was the product of a delusion. The guilty decision was based on his detailed awareness of the criminality of his act and the clever methods he used to escape detection. Shaykh al-Leḥaidān makes a strong point of whether the condition was inherited or not. In reality, psychiatrists are unable to make the clinical distinction between the two. Also, the issue of partial responsibility arises here; it is one that merits much further reflection and debate.

CASE 9

Criminal responsibility of a mentally ill person committing an act not prompted by his illness

A twenty-one-year-old was diagnosed schizophrenic less than a year ago. He had experimented with all kinds of illegal drugs for over four years, since high school. Since his illness he had been suffering from delusions and hallucinations, but had continued to abuse drugs. One day he decided to rob a pharmacy in order to get hold of some drugs. He actually did so, was arrested and brought before the court. His family and lawyer claimed that he was not guilty by reason of insanity.

The prosecution argued that his mental illness was totally unrelated to the nature of the crime he committed, namely theft. Being mentally ill is not an excuse because the accused had used drugs habitually long before the onset of his mental illness.

Question
Which of the claims is right? The man really is mentally ill and could be called insane, but his criminal action had nothing to do with, and did not stem from, his mental illness.

Answer
To say he "could be called insane" does not sufficiently identify the condition. The answer is limited to the amount of information:

If it was medically proven, even with 50% reliability, that the accused was mentally disturbed during his action, he should get a lighter punishment, and he cannot have his hand amputated according to the *ḥadd* punishment for theft because of the element of doubt. He should then be sent for compulsory treatment but the request for such commitment should come from the guardian, next of kin or his clan.

I do not see any relationship between the nature of his crime and his mental illness, but the state of insanity is a factor in reducing the sentence.

Comment
In secular law this person would most likely be found guilty. The secular law makes the distinction between the existence of mental illness and the nature of the crime. In this case, the crime is totally independent of the nature of the mental illness of the accused who is then expected to carry full legal responsibility for it. Shaykh al-Leḥaidān again raises the possibility of giving a lighter sentence. The fact of mental illness put a shadow of doubt on the degree of

culpability so that the *ḥadd* could not be applied. The issue of partial responsibility is again raised in this example.

CASE 10
Competence to stand trial

The police department in a large city discovered a dead body at the side of a road. After several months of investigation, a foreign laborer was charged with the crime. After arrest, it became clear that the accused man was not mentally stable. He was then sent to a psychiatric hospital to determine his state of mind and his criminal responsibility. The psychiatric report confirmed a mental illness and that the accused was currently insane. However, it was impossible to determine whether he had been insane during the execution of the crime. He was also declared incompetent to stand trial because unable to understand the nature of the charges against him. From the history taken from the accused's employer and other people who knew him, it was clear that he had been in sound mental health several months ago and may have been so also during the execution of the crime.

Question
Which of the following decisions would be the correct one?

1. The accused should be tried and if found guilty, should be sentenced by the judge. The rule of insanity would not apply since he was not insane at the time of the crime.
2. If tried and found guilty, he should not be sentenced because he is currently insane.
3. He cannot be tried because he is unable to defend himself and cannot comprehend the nature of the charges. He cannot discuss and argue his case with the judge and the witnesses. He should be committed for treatment.
4. Trial should be indefinitely postponed until the accused has been treated and declared competent.

Answer
The answer most likely to be correct is the first. The accused, if found guilty by reliable adult witnesses beyond reasonable doubt, should

be sentenced and receive the Shariʿah punishment, because he was not insane at the time the crime was committed.

If there are no reliable witnesses, the accused should be sent for treatment and if he recovers he should then be tried afterwards.

In my personal opinion, whether the mental illness was acquired or inherited is an important matter to consider, in order to reach a conclusion based on Shariʿah principles.

Comment

In this example the issue of competence to stand trial was raised. Under secular law conventions this person's mental illness would render him incompetent to face the court. Shaykh al-Leḥaidān does not recognize the accused's present incompetence to stand trial as a factor if the crime is satisfactorily proven by witnesses and evidences. The trial is delayed only if there are no reliable witnesses or evidences, requiring the accused to be competent in order to be questioned by the court.

CASE 11

Competence for execution

A forty-seven-year-old man killed one of the residents of a house he was trying to rob. He was tried, convicted and sentenced to death. Before he was executed, he became febrile and was sent to a hospital. He was diagnosed with cerebrospinal meningitis. He was treated for a period of time but left with serious and permanent brain damage. He had lost most of his cognitive functions, was unable to recognize his immediate relatives, completely disoriented and had suffered serious memory loss.

Question

1. Should the death sentence be carried out because the man was completely sane and competent at the time of his crime as well as during the trial and conviction? Or does his present state render him incompetent to be executed because he cannot now comprehend the nature of his crime, the reason for his execution?

2. Assuming that the brain damage he suffered, though severe, nevertheless left him able to recall his crime and to understand the meaning of the punishment he is receiving, does the presence of mental illness make him incompetent to be executed, or does the residual mental ability he has in the form of understanding the reason for the punishment render him competent to be executed?

Answer

An accused person can also suffer serious mental or emotional disorder as a consequence of the process of interrogation and confession.

In answer to the question: the convicted and condemned person must be executed, because the *ḥadd* is based on what happened before and during the crime, not after it.

We should, however, look at every case individually and study the events and the circumstances of the robbery and murder. The nature of the mental illness should be evaluated precisely so we can make a better judgment.

Comment

The Islamic jurists of the past had differing views on the issue of competence for execution. Some thought that if a person was sane during the act and the trial he should be executed, much like the opinion given here. Others felt differently. (See above, p. 53 for an account of the different arguments and opinions).

CASE 12
'Retrograde Amnesia'

A twenty-six-year-old robbed a high street bank and then tried to get away in a car. During the police car chase that followed, the getaway car struck a lamppost and the driver suffered a severe head injury. After recovering from the head injury, he was physically as well as mentally healthy except for one problem. He had 'retrograde amnesia': he had forgotten all the events just before the accident including the bank robbery itself. Retrograde amnesia is a recognized medical condition in which the patient forgets all events that happened during, and for the few hours, before his head injury. The psychiatrist cannot prove that this condition did not occur.

Question

1. Can the man be tried in the normal way and, if found guilty, given the *ḥadd* punishment? Or is he incompetent to be tried because of his amnesia of the relevant events? He would be unable to argue his case and defend himself before the judge, or to examine the evidence against him or communicate with witnesses to the events of the crime. Can he be considered incompetent to be tried on account of his amnesia?
2. There is another approach, whereby the accused is filled in on all the events of the crime to a point where he would have a significant idea about those circumstances, so that he can be considered competent to stand trial. Is this approach valid in your opinion?

Answer

Before the Shariʿah punishment can be pronounced, several facts have to established: that the stolen money was lawful property; that it was valued above the minimal amount; that it was unlawfully taken from a closed place; that the thief was an adult and sane. What happens after the events is irrelevant.

There is another point that arises from the circumstances of this case. The fact that the man was injured after or during a police chase might make the police partly liable. The police chase must have been conducted in a professional manner, and the policemen must have received proper training in carrying out such chases.

As for the judgment on the accused: it should be carried out in the normal way irrespective of his memory problem.

Comment

A more involved example of the competence to stand trial issue. The cognitive and intellectual functions of the accused are all quite normal. He can understand the nature of the case against him, participate in his defense with a counsel. However, he cannot remember the facts of the case in question. A similar case was presented in court in the United States, where the approach outlined in the second question was followed: the accused was given a detailed account of the case so that he could take part in his defense.

The Shaykh's answer, like his answer to an earlier question, gave no recognition to the concept of competence to stand trial: presumably he saw the circumstances as leaving little room for the accused to claim innocence.

CASE 13
'Fugue state' and other disassociative disorders

Khalid is an eighteen-year-old man who has just returned to his home country after eight years studying in the West. He has experienced many psychological problems. He came back home in a distressed emotional state, his use of Arabic seriously impaired, and with difficulties facing up to the demands of everyday life.

One day, without telling anyone, Khalid took a flight to another part of the country. At the airport he made advances to one of the flight attendants, to the point of actually attacking her. He was arrested. The following day in jail, he abruptly began making claims to the effect that he did not know where he was and that he had no recollection of any of the events of the last few days. He had no memory of leaving his home or indeed even his bedroom. When examined by a psychiatrist, he was diagnosed as having a 'fugue state'.

Fugue state is a rare psychiatric disorder. The patient usually has no apparent symptoms nor complains of any. The effect of this disorder is that the patient, for no apparent reason, travels, or does other things that he would not normally do, but rarely a heinous criminal act. After such episodes the patient has no memory of the events or of the acts he committed during these episodes. The fugue state is a disturbance in consciousness. It is not considered a psychotic state. The patient is not considered medically insane in these conditions.

Question

1. Can Khalid be held responsible for his actions if he was not conscious of them?

2. Can he be judged responsible because his disorder is not psychotic and can not justify the insanity defense?
3. Can Khalid be put on trial, because his memory loss about the events in question prevents him from offering an adequate defense?

Answer

Please refer to my book *Ḥāl al-Muttaham fī Majlis al-Qaḍā'* (The State of the Accused in an Islamic Court).[1] Whether Khalid was responsible for his action or not will depend on the nature of his condition.

If his disorder is an inherited condition, then it will be circumstantial evidence to be taken into account [i.e., a mitigating factor]. Or it may be an acquired condition. The psychiatrist making the diagnosis should be a person of integrity and an expert in his profession, one who can identify malingerers. We should also look at the accused's past criminal record if any. In general, it seems that Khalid should receive a lighter sentence, because of his disorder. Information from the witnesses will give a lot of clues as to the accused's state of mind at the time of the act.

Comment

This example brings a rare but interesting condition like 'fugue state' for discussion. The fact that he was not conscious of his action would appear to make him not guilty. However, the Shaykh takes the middle position and holds the accused partially responsible, and suggests a lighter sentence. He made no comment on the question about the competence of the accused to stand trial.

CASE 14
'Irresistible impulse' or 'inability to refrain'

Maḥmūd, a thirty-seven-year-old man, was suffering from severe mood swings and problems holding his temper. He was, nevertheless, known to be a responsible person at home and liked by his friends. He was a high school graduate and worked as a clerk in a government office. He had a lot of marital problems, mostly arising from his bad temper and loss of control in his behavior with his wife. Because of these mood swings and his tendency to be depressed, he sought treatment from a psychiatrist. But his disorder is not considered a mental illness. At one point he was admitted to a hospital for treatment of his depression. He spent some time there and was doing well and about to be discharged. However, while in hospital, a visitor came to him with some upsetting news. He informed Maḥmūd that his wife was having an affair and that there was a strange man in his house at that moment. In an outraged state, Maḥmūd rushed out of hospital, with-out being discharged, and headed directly to his house. There, he found his wife in light clothing. Although there was no man in the house, he was unable to control himself, and lost his senses at the sight of his wife in light clothing. He began to beat her and continued until she actually died.

Question

1. Is Maḥmūd criminally responsible for his action because, although he was under psychiatric care, he was not suffering from a mental illness?
2. Or, is he regarded as not criminally responsible because he was in an extreme state of rage and acted on an impulse from which he could not refrain?

Answer

The question here is presumably limited to the case of this particular individual. It is my view that whoever told him about his wife should carry his share of the responsibility because he had a role in the sequence of events. That person may have been ignorant or mentally disturbed himself, or had a malicious intent.

Maḥmūd has killed an innocent person because of his paranoia that was caused by:

1. the news about his wife's infidelity;
2. his psychiatric illness;
3. his bad temperament.

So, if his psychiatric condition really was as described, and his mind was in the state as described during the criminal act, he would be eligible for a lighter sentence. The news he received was a factor aggravating his pre-existing psychiatric condition.

Comment

This case was derived from a real event that took place in a Muslim country. It illustrates the concept of 'inability to refrain'. Under a secular law the accused would most likely be found not guilty because he was in a state where he could not refrain from his act due to the intensity of the situation, the predisposition of his personality and psychiatric problems. The answer presented here indicates a middle position, where the Shaykh could not find him not guilty and at the same time suggested the possibility of a lighter sentence. The 'inability to refrain' rule is recognized in many, but not all, states in the United States, and in Europe.

CASE 15
Unconsented administration of medication

Paranoia is a rather common disorder that burdens the sufferer with unfounded suspicions that people are out to hurt him. It can sometimes take the form of pathological jealousy, as unjustly suspecting a wife or husband of being unfaithful.

Sufferers do not recognize their delusions to be without substance, and therefore most of them refuse treatment. Most likely victims of such patients are wives who are frequently unfairly accused and abused by their paranoid husbands.

Question

Can the psychiatrist prescribe medication for the patient, without his knowledge and consent, and have the wife secretly put it in the man's drink or food? This medication is usually very effective in treating the condition. Further, it does not affect the person so as to make him uncaring about his wife's behavior, that is to say, it does not affect normal reaction to a situation that might really be a cause of jealousy.

Answer

If the case is medically proven and the medication has no alcohol in it, then doing this is approved.

Also, the wife must learn how to be more forbearing. This in itself is a kind of treatment. Secondly, the husband may be convinced by reading the Qur'an. And thirdly, he may be treated by companionship, such as a relative or friend who is a mature adult and can act as an advisor and a helping mind for him.

This is a common problem, but reading the Qur'an (which is the ideal treatment) is seldom used; the wife and her relatives can make the problem worse by not being understanding.

Comment

This an example of many cases psychiatrists in the Islamic world encounter. The wives have to suffer from their husband's unfair accusations which are commonly due to paranoid delusions. The delusion may be mild and noticeable by wives only. That is why these men can pass as normal in their communities. At King Faisal Specialist Hospital we have been able to obtain a fatwa from Shaykh al-ʿUthaymīn allowing the wife to put anti-psychotic medication in her husband's drink or food, thus keeping peace and quiet in the household. The issue here is patient consent for treatment. In the Islamic perspective, the right to treatment and care overrides the patient's right to refuse medications.

CASE 16
When a mentally ill person had a choice

Na'if is a thirty-one-year-old schizophrenic whose condition has been vacillating between remission and relapse, as his delusions and hallucinations change in intensity. At one point he was well and functioning at a satisfactory level, working and taking care of his family's needs. At the same time, however, he was having delusions and nightmares that he was keeping to himself. His delusions were that his cousin, who lived in the neighborhood, hated him and was plotting to kill him. These delusions were centered around the idea that his cousin believed that Na'if had planted drugs in his car as a result of which the cousin had been arrested and served a prison sentence. In reality Na'if had never done such a thing nor did his cousin believe that he had. One day, Na'if went ahead and killed his cousin to avoid being targeted by him according to his delusions. He executed the murder in a sophisticated way, with attempts to avoid being suspected.

Question
Which of the following decisions is more likely to be correct?

1. Na'if is not considered responsible for his action because he is mentally ill and was acting through the effect of delusions.
2. Na'if is responsible for his action. He knew that his action was not legal, and he would be punished if convicted, as is evident from his attempts to conceal the crime. One might argue that he was acting in self-defense albeit based on his delusions. But the fact is that he killed the cousin without seeking less violent means of dealing with the situation, such as talking to a friend, or filing a complaint with the local police and asking them for protection. Had he been ignored by the police, his action might have been considered a kind of self-defense.

Answer
The preferred answer is the second, and for the very reasons stated. I disagree on the last statement made: his action could not be considered self-defense under any circumstances.

Comment
This case illustrates the need to prove that less drastic measures must be taken before the extreme of killing can be justified as self defense. Granted the accused was acting out of delusions, he should at least have tried to protect himself by more appropriate methods, like calling the police, or asking someone else to help him.

CASE 17
Acting beyond the demands of delusions

Ḥasan is a thirty-eight-year-old schizophrenic suffering from delusions and hallucinations about his neighbor. He thought his neighbor was spying on him, became obsessed with these thoughts and decided to put an end to the harassment he felt was coming from that neighbor. He followed the man and killed him. He was arrested and his case was presented for psychiatric evaluation. The psychiatrist decided that Ḥasan did have a genuine mental illness that can cause a state of insanity at times. The psychiatrist indicated that the accused was a highly intelligent person in spite of the delusions he had about his neighbor. He also stated that Ḥasan had reported that his neighbor was intending to blackmail him about something. Ḥasan was fully aware that killing someone is a crime punishable by law. He had executed the crime with a lot of care in an effort to leave no clues that would lead to his arrest. The fact that he went to great lengths to avoid being discovered and arrested means, from the legal point of view, that he was fully aware of the wrongfulness of his act.

Question
Which of these opinions is correct?

1. Ḥasan is not held to be responsible for his action because he is mentally ill. He acted directly in response to his delusion, a fact supported by the expert psychiatric opinion.
2. Ḥasan is held to be responsible for his action because, granted he is mentally ill and acting out of delusion, he knew that his action was punishable and against the law. As for his action being a product of a delusion, his delusion, however real to him, did not call for murder: he was only annoyed by his neighbor's spying on him and he never thought his life was in danger. Ḥasan's intelligence was normal, therefore he was expected to act in a more reasonable way assuming his neighbor was indeed about to black mail him. He could have called the police, for example, or tried to confront the neighbor, instead of planning and carrying out his murder.

Answer
As the answer in the previous case. The second judgement is the right one.

Comment

This case example is based on one given in a forensic psychiatry course in the United States. It illustrates the fact that, granted mental illness might be present, and the criminal action taken was probably a direct result of a delusion, the action must follow a reason prompted by the delusion. In this case, the action taken was not called for by the nature of the delusion, therefore the accused was found guilty.

CASE 18
Impulse control disorder

Qāsim is a nineteen-year-old known to be suffering from impulse control disorder. If he tries to resist his impulses, it causes him a lot of mental anguish and stress. He derives pleasure from these unhealthy impulses as well as enjoying the relief he feels from indulging them. These impulses are that he must touch women on their clothes, close to the genital area. He has been able to escape punishment several times, because it is difficult to prove these kinds of assaults and because women are usually too embarrassed to report them. One day he was caught in the act and presented to court. Qāsim pleaded not guilty, presenting a psychiatric report indicating that he was afflicted with this kind of impulse disorder.

Question

Which of the following decisions is more likely to be right?

1. Qāsim is not guilty because he was acting out of an impulse caused by a psychiatric disorder, and his criminal action was of the same nature as his psychiatric disorder.
2. Qāsim is responsible for his action and should receive the appropriate punishment because he was able to tell right from wrong. He could have refrained from the act he committed. The worst he would have suffered, had he refrained, is some mental distress. That is not a sufficient reason for him to let his impulses go uncontrolled.

Answer

My judgement is that the person is responsible and should be tried as such. He should also receive treatment at the same time. Both punishment and treatment are important to make that person aware of the problem and not to let him use his illness as an excuse. His illness might persist for a time but that does not mean he may impose on others. To my knowledge this disorder requires an early deterrent. Deterrents should be effective in getting rid of this kind of behavior.

Comment
An example of non-psychotic impulse control disorder, like the condition of compulsive rapists or kleptomaniacs. These are cases where the law does not recognize a mere psychiatric disorder as a reason for acquittal. This is usually the position of the secular law, and Islamic law apparently takes a similar stand.

CASE 19
'Alcoholic dementia'

A sixty-five-year-old used to have an alcohol habit. He stopped it some years ago. Whether he did so repentant of his sin of drinking or for other reasons, it is not clear. As he entered his sixties he started to suffer from what was diagnosed as 'alcoholic dementia'. This condition is a kind of impairment in memory, orientations and other cognitive functions. He was no longer able to distinguish between right and wrong because his intelligence was significantly impaired. This condition was caused by his earlier consumption of alcohol, the brain damage was permanent and there is no treatment for it.

One day the old man exposed himself to a girl in the neighborhood. The girl's family pressed charges.

Question
Which of the following decisions is more acceptable?

1. The man has done a horrible thing and must be punished for it as the judge sees fit. The fact that he is brain damaged is not a reasonable defense because that condition was caused by his drinking, which he did of his own will. There is no excuse for an action that was done under the effect of a substance that was willingly and knowingly taken.

2. The man is not responsible for his action because of the mental impairment caused by alcoholic dementia. The fact that alcohol was taken willingly many years ago is not a reason for him to be considered culpable, because, when he was drinking alcohol, he did not know about the possible dementia. We must assume that he has repented of his sin of drinking and that he was trying to avoid the consequences.

Answer
If the fact that he stopped drinking a long time ago is as stated, and the fact was supported by medical evaluation, the old man is not liable. He should, however, be treated and controlled to avoid problems.

Comment
In spite of the harsh view of Islamic teaching on alcohol, the position taken by the Shaykh is very similar to that of the secular law. Usually the secular law will find alcoholic dementia a reasonable ground for acquittal. At the same time acute alcoholic intoxication is not a recognized defense against any action done during the intoxication.

CASE 20
'Delirium tremens'

Zayd is a fifty-year-old man who has been a heavy drinker for many years. One day he started to suffer from symptoms of agitation, anxiety, trembling, and mental confusion. These symptoms were diagnosed as 'delirium tremens' a kind of withdrawal symptoms that start to evolve between one or fourteen days from the cessation of alcohol consumption. Zayd had been off alcohol for about two weeks when these symptoms started to develop. When Zayd was confused and hallucinating he got aggressive and agitated and would hit out at random. On one such occasion he caused a serious head injury to a person close enough to get hit. Zayd was taken to hospital and eventually fully recovered. The injured person pressed charges.

Question
Which decision is more likely to be correct?

1. Zayd is considered liable for his action. In spite of the fact that he was mentally incompetent at the time of the injury he caused, the temporary state of mental impairment was self-induced by voluntary consumption of alcohol. The customary rule is that an individual is fully responsible for his action, when he is under the influence of any mind-altering substance, if it was consumed voluntarily.
2. Zayd is not legally responsible because, at the time of the act, he had been off alcohol for two weeks. Also he had no knowledge of this kind of withdrawal symptoms. As to the fact that he had committed a sinful act by consuming alcohol, this might not be admissible because he had stopped drinking two weeks before. He might, at least in principle, have decided on repentance.
3. He is not responsible for his action for the reasons just given. However, if he ever drinks again and ends up in a similar condition, he could not be excused. The fact that he had no knowledge of the symptoms of late withdrawal was the point that rendered him inculpable.

Answer

These kinds of issues have been discussed and argued by many Islamic judges and scholars under the title of "divorce under the influence of alcohol." Some have argued that divorce is not valid if it is pronounced by a drunken man. Others insisted that the divorce is valid because the man has committed the act of consumption of alcohol on his own volition and he should bear the consequences of his action.

A case like Zayd's should be looked at in a similar way, to avoid making alcohol a pretext for avoiding the legal responsibility for divorce or for criminal acts.

Comment

A similar case was discussed among doctors. The consensus was that it is unreasonable to expect the public to know about the nature of delirium tremens. Therefore, the third decision was preferred. As the person now knows what delirium tremens can lead to, he is expected to refrain from alcohol; if he does not, he is liable for the consequences.

CASE 21
Involuntary treatment of a physically ill but mentally healthy person

A forty-two-year-old patient, suffering permanent and complete renal failure, has become dependent for survival on dialysis at least twice a week. The patient became so distressed and annoyed with the dialysis machine that he decided one day to refuse treatment altogether. Medical staff explained to him that not to continue treatment would mean certain death. The only way he could survive is through regular dialysis till an appropriate transplant became available.

It is important to note that this patient has no psychiatric illness and is mentally competent.

Question
If he continues to refuse medical treatment can the physician or members of the patient family force him to be treated against his will, and without his consent, to save his life?

Answer
I am sorry I seem unable to answer this question.

Comment
The Shaykh did not clarify his reasons for not commenting on this situation.

This issue was discussed under the topic 'the concept of patient consent in Islamic law' (see above, pp.30–32). Opinions vary and scholars have given different rulings on the issue of involuntary treatment of a patient who is mentally competent and not suffering from any psychiatric disorder. The opinion of the majority was that it is acceptable to force the patient to accept treatment if it is life saving.

CASE 22
Contested divorce of a dying patient

A seventy-two-year-old man, who had a heart attack later complicated by chronic heart failure, suffered from this illness for thirteen months before he finally died of it. After the onset of his illness, he was increasingly unhappy about his wife's attitude. She seemed to him not to want to be bothered with his care, nor to cater to his needs. He divorced her two months after he became ill. After his death, his wife protested the divorce and demanded her share of the inheritance. She maintained that the divorce was not valid because it took place during the husband's illness that eventually led to his death. The man died eleven months after the divorce and was mentally competent.

Question
Is the divorce in this condition valid, in spite of its occurrence during the illness that about a year later led to death, bearing in mind that the deceased enjoyed sound mental health till the end of his life?

Answer
The divorce is definitely valid. The wife is legally divorced. However, if the problem here is in her right of inheritance, then it would depend on the man's intention. If there is evidence that by divorcing her he was intending to deprive her of the inheritance, then she will inherit from him as if she had not been divorced. But if there is no evidence that by divorcing her he intended to deprive her of her inheritance, rather that he really did not want her as a wife and that this was his only reason for the divorce, then she will not inherit from him.

The divorce in any case is valid.

Comment
This question reflects the confusion created by the act of a person during an illness that leads to death. Many scholars believe that an action like divorce, if taken during an illness that leads to death, is not considered effective in causing any alteration of the inheritance right. Evidently, this action is only invalid if it was intended to deprive an heir of inheritance. As in this example, the wife's right of the inheritance, even though she was divorced legally, is preserved, if she can demonstrate that her ex-husband's intention was to deprive her of the inheritance. This illustrates the minimal power of a will in Islamic law.

CASE 23
Contested sale contract of a dying patient

A sixty-year-old man died after sixteen months of struggling with viral hepatitis. A year before his death he sold a building he owned to help pay for his health bills. After his death, his heirs contested the sale because it was carried out during the man's illness that led to his death. Also the building was worth more than one-third of the man's whole wealth.

Question

Was the sale of that building really invalid, because it took place during the illness of the deceased, bearing in mind that the value of the building exceeds one-third of the man's total wealth, and that he was in sound mental health till the end of his life.

Answer

In a case like this, questions should be asked about what role the heirs played during the deceased's illness. Did they stand by him and support him?

As for the sale, it is valid as long as it was done in the right legal way. There was a mutual agreement and both the buyer and the seller were mature adults, and mentally competent. If, however, it was found that the building was sold for far less than its worth, then a committee of experts should go out and assess the situation. The whole issue is then evaluated in court.

The fact that the building was sold at the time of illness that led to death is irrelevant, because that is God's judgment. This case is an example of what heirs frequently try to do to contest the invalidity of a sale.

Comment

The answer given by the Shaykh indicates the confusion in people's minds about the validity of any action taken by a person during an illness that ended in death. Many believe that a person during a sickness that leads to death cannot deal with a property that exceeds the amount of one-third of his total wealth. Obviously this is not necessarily true, in the light of the answer here.

CASE 24

Contested will of a dying person within one-third of total wealth

A seventy-year-old was diagnosed with cancer of the pancreas. At that age there is no effective treatment known for this condition. During the last six months of his life and after he realized the nature of his disease, he wrote his will. He gave one-third of his total wealth to his long orphaned nephews. After his death, his sons protested the will, insisting that it could not be valid because it had been written during the illness that led to death.

Question

Is the will valid? Given the fact that the testator was mentally competent during the writing of the will.

Answer

In general it is valid, but many issues should be considered, for example:

1. Is the handwriting on the document that of the man, or of someone authorized by him; have the heirs contested the handwriting?
2. Have the man's integrity and piety ever been questioned?
3. Were there any problems between him and his children during his life?

If doubts of that kind are proven true, the will could be contested, and the judge should study the matter fully and in detail.

If none of the doubts is true, the will is valid.

Comment

Another example of the value of a will written during an illness that led to death. Here the man has not violated the rule of not giving away more than one-third of his total wealth to non-heirs. (In Islamic law you are not allowed to will more than one-third of the total wealth.) Yet, the children still found grounds to contest it. The answer indicates that, if there were evidence of personal problems between the deceased and his heirs, his right of disposal of even less than one-third of his total wealth can be contested.

It is important to note that in matters relating to illness that leads to death, the issue of intention is the central concern. That is to say, whether or not the testator was intending to deprive an heir of his or her share. Since evaluating intention is a matter that requires some psychological expertise, psychiatrists can expect to be more involved in these matters.

CASE 25
Competence to confess

Ṣāliḥ is a twenty-two-year old schizophrenic patient, attended by a psychiatrist for many years. One day a corpse was discovered in the neighborhood where Ṣāliḥ lived. While the police were investigating the incident, Ṣāliḥ came to them and confessed to the act. He gave his reason as having to obey commands received from heaven. Since Ṣāliḥ was known to be mentally ill, the police were hesitant to accept his confession at face value. Subsequently, Ṣāliḥ retracted his confession.

Question
Which of the following processes is most appropriate?

1. Ṣāliḥ should be ignored. His confession has no value due to his known mental illness. The psychiatrist has testified that he is suffering from hallucinations and delusions.
2. Ṣāliḥ should be tried, without giving weight to his confession, because he is not competent to confess. If he is found to have commited the act, he should be sent for treatment rather than punishment because he was not mentally competent to appreciate the nature of his act. However, if the insanity defence is found be inapplicable, he is to be sentenced as any other individual.
3. If the psychiatrist confirms Ṣāliḥ as not only incompetent to make a confession, but also to understand the nature of the accusation and the court proceedings and to assist counsel in his defense, he is then considered incompetent to stand trial. He should be sent for treatment, while postponing the trial till he is competent. If he becomes competent to stand trial, he should then be tried and the procedures followed as in (2.)

Answer
According to the description of the case, the accused seems to be insane and cannot be culpable. But does the accused have any prior criminal record? And, are there witnesses, or circumstantial evidence like fingerprints, etc. At any rate, I would suggest the second procedure.

Comment
The purpose of this question was to bring into discussion the issue of 'competence to confess'. A similar point was discussed in a meeting of the American Academy of Psychiatry and Law in San Antonio, Texas, in October 1993, where it was felt that the proper procedure to follow was as under (3.) That is competence to stand trial as well as competence to make a confession must both be affirmed before the person is tried.

Shaykh al-Leḥaidān, as in previous answers, chose not to eval-uate the need for competence to stand trial, before a trial could be conducted.

CASE 26
Mother's fitness for custody when the father is psychiatrically unfit

A woman was divorced from her husband upon her insistence. Her husband persistently abused alcohol and drugs over many years. The woman had been married to this irresponsible man for many years, and tried all avenues and sought advice from *ʿulamāʾ*, but she had been unable to keep her husband away from drugs and alcohol.

The issue is that she has a nine-year-old daughter, and the husband is insisting that she live with him under his care and custody. The girl does not want to leave her mother because she knows about her father's ways. The father's only reason for wanting the child with him is to punish her mother.

The woman refused to turn over her daughter to her ex-husband because he is an alcoholic and because she is better able to take care of her child than him.

Question
Can the mother in this case keep her daughter till she gets married? The mother here is evidently wiser and more intelligent and better

able to give proper care to the daughter than the father. Also, the mother was able to present a psychiatric report documenting her husband's alcoholic problem.

Answer
If it is proved that the mother is better in her religion and honesty than the father, she should have custody. There is no disagreement to my knowledge between Islamic jurists on this issue, even after the residential custody period has passed. This is what is being done in the Islamic world now. The best interest of the girl is with her mother, if it is established that the mother is religiously and behaviorally more qualified than the father.

Comment
The father's right to have full custody of his daughter when she attains seven or nine years of age (depending on the scholarly school) goes uncontested most of the time. The Shaykh's answer indicates that this right can be contested by the mother if the father is seen to be unfit for behavioral or psychiatric reasons.

CASE 27
Expert opinion on the best interest of the child

A couple who got divorced had two children, a four-year-old son and a ten-year-old daughter. The man spent most of the years of his marriage going from one country to another on business. He was rarely home, so his wife was doing all the duties of both mother and father. She is an educated woman, so she would take her children to school and help them with their homework. She has devoted every part of her life to her children and never pursued a career herself in order to be always available to her children. Naturally, the children grew up strongly attached to their mother, especially because their father was rarely home. The father, in addition to his frequent travels, did not spend time with his wife and children even when he was in town. He preferred the company of his friends and would spend many nights with his male friends. The children, after the divorce, refused to go with their father and stayed with the mother. The father asked the judge to have his children with him against their will. The mother protested and pointed out that their mental health would suffer if they were to be forced to live with him. She supported her claim by presenting a psychiatrist's report indicating that the best interest of the children was to remain with their mother. They are attached to her and she has proved herself all these years to be a suitable and appropriate parent for them.

Question

Which of the following judgements is most appropriate?

1. The girl should go to her father and the boy stay with the mother if he chooses.
2. Satisfying the criterion of the best interests of the child will follow the psychiatrist recommendation – that the children stay with the mother till the girl gets married and the boy makes his choice.
3. Ensure that the psychiatrist made a sound and unbiased judgment by calling for a second opinion from another psychiatrist of the judge's choice, then follow that decision. This is a viable solution because issues of custody are subject to many juristic and scholarly differences. The Shāfiʿī school for example let the boy or girl choose.
4. Give the choice and the decision to the children themselves.

Answer

It is mentioned here that the father spent many nights out. It is not clear whether that was spent in drinking and doing other evil things like neglecting prayer. If that is the case, the answer is clear much as in the question before. The mother is more appropriate because she is observing the religious duties. However, if that was not the case, and the father was just busy at work and socializing, then the girl should be with her father. The boy can have the choice between his mother or his father.

It is important here to note that since the mother has spent so much time and effort in fulfilling the duties of both the mother and the father, the father is ordered to pay the mother compensation for her hard work. The judge should decide on the kind and amount of this compensation.

Comment

In this case we attempted to test the principle of the best interest of the child as advised by the psychiatrist. It was pointed out that, unlike the previous case, the father was not seen as having extreme behavioral or psychiatric problems. The point stressed here is that the children's best interest, as seen by the psychiatrist, was to be with their mother. The Shaykh's answer was to disregard this advice and place the girl with the father. It is quite possible that Shaykh al-Leḥaidān has here followed the judgement typical of Ḥanbalī *fiqh*. It is possible that a judge schooled in Shāfiʿī *fiqh* would give a different ruling.

CASE 28
Child abused by his mother

A woman is suffering the rare and unusual psychiatric disorder called Munchausen's syndrome by proxy. This disorder is a dangerous one. Its danger affects the child or children and not the mother. It is difficult to diagnose because there are no clear signs and symptoms. It is only diagnosed after long and very careful observation of the mother and her behavior with the children. It is characterized by a strong and persistent tendency of the mother to hurt her children. This activity can lead to death in a very subtle way. Known regimes of treatment for this condition are of very questionable value. The only way to manage the danger to the children is to have the children removed from the mother.

This woman lost her first child because she had regularly poured bleach down the baby's throat. The doctor did not suspect the mother as the perpetrator and had misdiagnosed the case. It was when the woman presented her second child with the identical strange symptoms and signs of changes in the throat that the doctor began to suspect the mother. He set about carefully monitoring the child's condition and observing the mother. He soon documented that the mother was putting bleach down her second baby's throat. The child needed to be taken away from the mother. The father refused to divorce the mother.

Question
Is it feasible to go to an Islamic court and ask the judge to remove the right of custody from the mother and give it to another person, in spite of the fact that the parents are living together?

Answer
If the case is proven true, custody should be moved to the maternal grandmother of the child, if she is living, otherwise to the paternal grandmother, maternal aunt and so on, according to the rules for the transition of custody.

Other conditions apply:

1. Mother's visitations rights with supervision.
2. Keep other children from knowing the nature of the problem with their mother.
3. Keep treating the mother with Qur'anic reading, because mysterious diseases can be treated by Qur'anic reading if the conditions allow, i.e. if the mother was agreeable or amenable.

Comment
This is a unique situation that has not been addressed in Islamic jurisprudence. The circumstances described are based on a real case in a Saudi hospital. There is no legal precedent for taking custody away from the mother based on Munchausen's syndrome by proxy or other child abuse cases. We needed a documented opinion on this matter from a respected judge like Shaykh al-Leḥaidān.

CASE 29

Child witness and expert testimony as hearsay

A man was brought in accused of sexually abusing a four-year-old boy. There was some incriminating evidence against the man: some pieces of hair were found on the victim's body. The child was psychologically so disturbed that he needed special treatment by a psychiatrist. The police arrested the perpetrator after the descriptions given by the child to his treating psychiatrist.

At the trial, the psychiatrist suggested that the child's testimony should be listened to, to help support the case against the accused. It is known that a child cannot be a witness, but we have here an expert testimony by a psychiatrist who is going to prepare the child for his testimony. The psychiatrist can give an account of what he has understood from his child patient, in addition to his own expert testimony.

Question

1. Can the court accept the child testimony at least as part of the relevant evidence, rather than as a witness testimony?
2. Can the psychiatrist's account of what he was told by the child victim be accepted as testimony? In other words, can an exception be made to introduce hearsay evidence?

Answer

In cases like this one, several points need to be taken into consideration, like:

1. There is no record of previous animosity between the accused and the child's parents.
2. There is no record of previous animosity between the doctor and the accused, or between him and the child's parents.
3. The criminal record of the accused (if any) should be studied.

Otherwise, a child at this age cannot be a witness, and we cannot listen to him unless the incident was very recent. Similarly, the doctor's testimony cannot be accepted.

This kind of case is better dealt with by keeping the events private and secret. The doctor should have handled the matter in a wise way, trying to avoid any kind of litigation. He should have persuaded the boy's family to go along with this approach in order to avoid scandal.

The doctor's statement in this case cannot be accepted as a direct witness, only as a report about the incident.

Comment

The question was put to see if hearsay evidence could be accepted under sensitive and very special circumstances. Also to seek clarification on the weight and relevance of the psychiatrist as an expert witness in cases of child abuse and molestation.

CASE 30
Assisted suicide

A patient asked his doctor to end his suffering by giving him an overdose of sleeping pills that would terminate his life. The patient was suffering from a serious illness that caused him an unbearable amount of pain and there was no hope for a cure. The doctor was not well-versed in religious doctrine or law. So, out of compassion for the patient, he went ahead and gave him a fatal overdose. He did so, however, only after taking a written letter and recording a video documenting the patient's request and need to have his life ended. The patient also stated in the letter and the video that he was responsible and carried his own blood and that he was not demanding *diyyah* from the doctor, and that the doctor was forgiven and absolved of any punishment.

Question

Which of the following decisions is most appropriate?

1. The *ḥadd* for murder should be implemented according to the Shariʿah.
2. The *ḥadd* (the death penalty in this case) should be implemented, only under one circumstance, namely if the deceased's family or clan refuse the bloodwit.
3. The doctor has committed an illegal and religiously forbidden act. However, the *ḥadd* cannot be implemented. Rather, he should be given a discretionary punishment (*taʿzīr*) to be decided by the ruler or the judge. That is because the deceased has forgiven his killer and declined the right of *diyyah* as compensation. So *taʿzīr* is the only possible punishment. (This decision may be based on the fact that the deceased is the one first responsible for his debts. Debt is usually paid from the deceased's wealth and then, if that is not enough, the heirs should pay the rest. So the deceased has first right to the bloodwit, and if he has declined that, then the doctor is not under religious obligation to pay the bloodwit or to suffer the *ḥadd*.)

Answer
There is first a question about the competence of the doctor as a physician, and his knowledge and morals and how honest he is and if he is sound mentally. Also, is mercy killing a subject that was taught to him in medical school?

The Islamic Shariʿah states:

1. That a human being does not own his own life. Also God has said in the Qur'an: "...Do not kill yourselves; God is ever merciful to you" (4:29). So a man does not have the right to end his own life. How can he give himself the right to end somebody else's life? Killing anybody for any reason is forbidden.
2. God may miraculously cure any body or the patient might become adjusted to his life.

Therefore the doctor should be punished severely through a *taʿzīr*. The *taʿzīr* here might be severe enough to be an execution. Please refer to books like Ibn Qudāmah's *al-Mughnī Sharḥ Mukhtaṣar al-Khiraqī* and Ibn Qayyim al-Jawziyyah's *al-Ṭuruq al-Hikmiyyah*, for more information.

Comment
This question was obviously put to further study the Islamic legal perspective on assisted suicide and so-called 'mercy killing'. The issue was raised in the text under the heading 'Consented Termination of Life' (see above, p.101). The Shaykh very firmly indicated that an appropriate *taʿzīr* punishment is the right course, and that 'mercy killing' is still killing in the Islamic legal perspective.

CASE 31
Malpractice compensation

A doctor performed surgery on an unmarried woman's nose to remove the adenoids and correct the nasal septum. During the operation, the surgeon was inattentive, and complications following the procedure led to a permanent deformity of the nose. The woman sued for damages.

A committee confirmed that the damage to the nose was a result of ignorance and neglect on the part of the surgeon, i.e. malpractice was established.

Question
Will the compensation for the damage be the *diyyah* amount as the Shariʿah calculates it? Or can the amount of compensation be more or less than the *diyyah*, at the discretion of the judge or the governor?

Answer
God has said in the Qur'an "the nose for a nose", but here I do not think the ruling should be to cut off the doctor's nose. Because that ruling is applied only if there is strong hatred and animosity between the two parties. I fail to see this level of animosity here.

The *diyyah* should be taken from the doctor because the damage was caused by him. If the deformity is severe and involves more than the nose, an experienced judge, in consultation with two other judges like him, can decide on the case for more than the *diyyah* amount. If the damage is limited to the nose and surgical correction is not possible, the *diyyah* amount as it is must be granted.

Comment
This question was put to clarify the discussion in the text (see above p.106). The compensation for damages in malpractice cases is probably judged by the *diyyah* which is a fixed amount; compensation above that is not expected. The concept of punitive damages does not exist in the *diyyah* system.

CASE 32
Compensation for injury beyond the diyyah amount

A surgeon was called to hospital one night in order to perform an emergency operation. His car was hit by another car travelling at excessive speed on the wrong side of the road. The surgeon suffered serious injuries and his right hand had to be amputated. Upon recovery, he demanded compensation for the damage. The driver who caused the damage offered the amount equal to half the full *diyyah*. This amount is significantly low, considering that the victim of the injury is a surgeon who lost a hand, which is the source of his livelihood. The surgeon demanded much more than hat.

Question
Is the surgeon right to demand more? Can the judge increase the amount of *diyyah* according to the extent of the injury, its effect on the nature of the job performed and on the economic status of the victim?

Answer
Yes that is possible . . . but it has to be evaluated by a skilled physician with long experience in this field.

Comment
Here is an example of a case where the *diyyah* amount is varied. Unlike the previous case, here the Shaykh is willing to award the surgeon more than the set amount of *diyyah*. The Shaykh did not elaborate on how he reached this decision and whether it was supported by authority from the Qur'an or Sunnah.

CASE 33
Imposed marital separation on patients with HIV

When Ibrahim returned from one of his long trips abroad, he was extremely tired, weak and became bed-ridden. Shortly afterwards, he was hospitalized because of multiple infections, and, extensive testing established that he had contracted an HIV infection. His symptoms were treated and he was able to return to more or less normal life. It is known that this disease has no cure as yet, and that Ibrahim will therefore carry the virus probably for the rest of his life. The problem is that Ibrahim is a careless and irresponsible person who insists on having unprotected sex with his pregnant wife. His wife, too, is indifferent to the seriousness of the condition, despite being pregnant and aware that there is strong risk of transmitting the disease to her unborn child. The wife refuses to listen to the doctors' and nurses' warnings about having unprotected sex with her husband.

Question
In a case like this, can doctors or health officers, or the family of the

people involved, petition the judge or the court to have the husband and wife separated against their will, in order to protect the wife as well as the unborn child?

Answer
In a case like this, I do not see that the guardian can request a divorce. But they could be ordered to be separated. That could be done till a vaccine or other form of treatment is available. The husband in this condition should be educated about the risk involved. It is mentioned here that he is careless and irresponsible. This kind of person must be psychologically sick and needs treatment for that too.

Comment
We believe this to be a new concept in Islamic jurisprudence. The health officers in this case are requesting an order to have the husband forcibly prevented from having sex with his wife in order to protect the wife and/or the fetus. This is being requested also against the wishes of the wife. A case like this has faced more than one clinician in practice in a Muslim country. It is important to have a formal, written view of this matter published so that people are properly informed of it.

NOTES

AUTHOR'S INTRODUCTION

1 (ṢAAS) – *Ṣallā Allāhu 'alayhi wa sallam*. May the peace and blessings of God be upon him. Said whenever the name of Prophet Muḥammad is mentioned

INTRODUCTION

1 Rosner, R. , *Principles and Practise of Forensic Psychiatry* (New York: Chapman & Hall, 1996), p.7.

2 Al-Qaraḍāwī, Yūsuf, *Al-Madkhal li Dirāsah al-Sharīʿah al-Islāmiyyah* (Cairo: Maktabah Wahba, 1991) p.57.

3 Ibid.

4 *Mawsūʿah al-Ḥadīth al-Sharīf* (CD ROM, 1st issue, Kuwait: Sharikah Ṣakhar li al-Ḥāsib al-Ālī, 1996): Ibn Mājah, *Sunan*, Bāb al-Aḥkam, hadith no. 2331.

5 I have relied in this section on the account in Muḥammad Maḥmūd Hāshim, *al-Qaḍā' wa Niẓām al-Ithbāt fī al-Fiqh al-Islāmī wa al-Anẓimah al-Waḍʿiyyah* (Riyadh: ʿImādah Shu'ūn al-Maktabāt Jāmiʿah al-Malik Saʿūd, 1988), esp. pp.29–43.

6 Ibid.

NOTES TO CHAPTER 1

1 Stone, A. A., *Law, Psychiatry and Morality* (Washington DC: American Psychiatric Press, 1984), p.37.

2 Applebaum, P. S. and Gutheil, T. G., *Clinical Handbook of Psychiatry and the Law* (New York: McGraw-Hill Book Co., 1991), pp.4–6.

3 Ibid., pp.153–55.

4 Dawidoff, D., 'Some Suggestions to Psychiatrists for Avoiding Legal Jeopardy', *Archives General Psychiatry*, 29:5 (Nov. 1973), pp.699–701.

5 Simon, R. I., (ed.) *Clinical Psychiatry and the Law*, 2nd edn. (Washington DC: American Psychiatric Press, 1992), p.48.

6 Sadoff, R. L., *Forensic Psychiatry: A Practical Guide for Lawyers and Psychiatrists* (Springfield Ill.: Charles C. Thomas, 1988), p.52.

7 Mills, M. J, Sullivan, G. and Eth, S., 'Protecting Third Parties: A Decade after Tarasoff', *American Journal of Psychiatry*, 144:1 (Jan. 1987), pp.68–74.

8 Al-Shaykh Mubārak (Qays ibn Muḥammad), *al-Tadāwī wa al-Mas'ūliyyah al-Ṭibbiyyah fī*

al-Sharīʿah al-Islāmiyyah (Damascus: Maktabah al-Fārābī, 1991), pp.17–24.

9 Ibid.

10 Ibn Ḥanbal, *Musnad al-Imām Aḥmad* (Cairo: al-Maṭbaʿah al-Maymaniyyah, 1313 AH), vol.2, p.33.

11 Al-Bukhārī, *Ṣaḥīḥ al-Bukhārī bi Sharḥ Fatḥ al-Bārī* (Cairo: al-Maṭbaʿah al-Khayriyyah, 1951), vol.5, p.284.

12 Al-Qarāfī (Shihāb al-Dīn Abū al-ʿAbbās al-Ṣanhājī), *al-Furūq* (Beirut: ʿĀlam al-Kutub, n.d.), vol.2, p.207.

13 Al-Zarqā (al-Shaykh Aḥmad ibn Muḥammad), *Sharḥ al-Qawāʿid al-Fiqhiyyah* (Beirut: Dār al-Gharb al-Islāmī, 1403 AH), p.159.

14 Ibn Qāsim (ʿAbd al-Raḥmān ibn Muḥammad al-Āṣimī), *Ḥāshiyah ibn Qāsim ʿalā al-Rawḍ al-Murabbaʿ* (Cairo: al-ʿArabī Publishing, n.d.), vol.7, p.436.

15 Al-Nawawī (Abū Zakariyyā), *Rawḍat al-Ṭālibīn* (Damascus: Maṭbaʿah al-Maktab al-Islāmī li al-Ṭibāʿah wa al-Nashr, n.d.) vol.3, p.286.

16 Ibn ʿAbd al-Salām (Abū Muḥammad ibn ʿAbd al-ʿAzīz al-Shāfiʿī), *Qawāʿid al-Aḥkām fī Maṣāliḥ al-'Anām* (Cairo: Dār al-Sharq li al-Ṭibāʿah, 1388 AH), vol.1, p.66; Ibn Farḥūn (Ibrāhīm ibn ʿAlī al-Yaʿmurī), *Tabṣirah al-Ḥukkām fī Uṣūl al-Aqḍiyah wa Manāhij al-Āḥkām*, (1st edn., Cairo: al-Maṭbaʿah al-ʿĀmirah al-Sharafiyyah, 1301 AH), vol.2, p.231; al-Māwardī (Abū al-Ḥasan), *al-Aḥkām al-Sulṭāniyyah* (Beirut: Dār al-Kutub al-ʿIlmiyyah, 1982), p.256.

17 Al-Ṭaḥṭāwī (Aḥmad ibn Muḥammad ibn Ismāʿīl), *Ḥāshiyah al-Ṭaḥṭāwī ʿalā al-Durr al-Mukhtār* (Cairo: al-Maṭbaʿah al-ʿĀmirah, 1238 AH), vol.4, p.218; al-Aṣbaḥī (Mālik ibn Anas), *al-Mudawwanah al-Kubrā* (Cairo: Dār al-Fikr li al-Ṭibāʿah wa al-Nashr wa al-Tawzīʿ, 1978), vol.4, p.374; al-Sharbīnī (Muḥammad ibn Aḥmad), *Mughnī al-Muḥtāj fī Maʿrifah Maʿānī Alfāẓ al-Minhāj* (Cairo: Maṭbaʿah Muṣṭafā al-Bābī al-Ḥalabī, 1377 AH), vol.4, p.309; al-Bahūtī (Abū ʿAbd Allāh Muḥammad), *Kashshāf al-Qināʿ ʿalā Matn al-Iqnāʿ* (Cairo: Muḥammad Afandī Muṣṭafā, n.d.), vol.6, p.10.

18 Ibn al-Nujaym (Zayn al-ʿĀbidīn ibn Ibrāhīm), *al-Ashbāh wa al-Naẓā'ir* (Beirut: Dār al-Kutub al-ʿIlmiyyah, 1980), p.124.

19 Al-Anṭākī, (Dāwūd ibn ʿUmar al-Baṣīr), *Tadhkhirah Ūlī al-Albāb*, (Cairo: Maṭbaʿah Muṣṭafā al-Bābī al-Ḥalabī, 1951), vol.1, p.9.

20 Resnick, P. J., 'The Psychiatrist in Court' in Cavenar Jr., J. O., (ed.) *Psychiatry* (Philadelphia: Lippincotti, 1989), p.146.

21 Al-Qalyūbī (Shihāb al-Dīn Aḥmad), *Ḥāshiyatān ʿalā Minhāj al-Ṭālibīn* (Cairo: al-Bābī

al-Ḥalabī, 1956), vol.4, p.326.

22 Ibn Qayyim al-Jawziyyah (Shams al-Dīn), *al-Ṭuruq al-Ḥikmiyyah fī al-Siyāsah al-Sharʿiyyah* (Cairo: Maṭbaʿah al-Madanī, n.d.), p.129; Ibn Farḥūn, *Tabṣirah al-Ḥukkām*, vol.1, p.229; al-Shāfiʿī, *al-Risālah* (Cairo: Dār al-Turāth, 1973), p.324.

23 Ibn Farḥūn, *Tabṣirah al-Ḥukkām*, vol.1, p.229.

24 Al-Wanshirīsī (Abū al-ʿAbbās Aḥmad ibn Yaḥyā), *al-Miʿyār al-Muʿrib wa al-Jamiʿa al-Mughrib ʿan Fatāwā ʿUlamā' Afrīqiyyah wa al-Maghrib* (Beirut: Dār al-Gharb al-Islāmī, 1981), vol.10, p.17.

25 Qur'an 17:34.

26 *Mawsūʿah al-Ḥadīth al-Sharīf*: Muslim, *Ṣaḥīḥ*, *Kitāb al-Birr wa al-Ādāb*, no.4677.

27 *Mawsūʿah al-Ḥadīth al-Sharīf*: al-Bukhārī, *Ṣaḥīḥ, Bāb al-Ādāb*, no.6387.

28 Ibid.: Abū Dāwūd, *Sunan*, *Kitāb al-Ādāb*, no.4225.

29 Al-Haytamī (Ibn Ḥajar), *al-Zawājir ʿan Iqtirāf al-Kabā'ir* (Beirut: Dār al-Maʿrifah, 1987), p.74.

30 Ibid., p.68; Ibn Farḥūn, *Tabṣirah al-Ḥukkām*, vol.1, p.231.

31 Al-Ḥaṭṭāb (Abū ʿAbd Allāh), *Mawāhib al-Jalīl li Sharḥ Mukhtaṣar al-Khalīl* (Cairo: Maṭbaʿah al-Saʿādah, 1328 AH), vol.6, p.164; Ibn Mufliḥ (Abū ʿAbd Allāh al-Maqdisī), *al-Ādāb al-Sharʿīyyah wa al-Minaḥ al-Marʿīyyah* (Riyadh: Maktabah al-Riyāḍ al-Ḥadīthah, 1391 AH), vol.1, p.263; al-Nawawī, *Sharḥ Ṣaḥīḥ Muslim*, (1st edn., Cairo: al-Maṭbaʿah al-Miṣriyyah, 1346 AH), vol.6, p.135.

32 Al-Zarkashī, *al-Manthūr min al-Qawāʿid*, (Kuwait: Maṭbaʿah Mu'assassah al-Fulayj li al-Ṭibāʿah wa al-Nashr, 1882), vol.1, p.189. Ibn Farḥūn, *Tabṣirah al-Ḥukkām*, vol.2, p.209.

NOTES TO CHAPTER 2

1 Rosner, *Principles and Practice of Forensic Psychiatry*, p.198.

2 Walker, N., *Crime and Insanity in England*, vol. 1: *The Historical Perspective* (Edinburgh: Edinburgh University Press, 1968), p.59.

3 Rosner (ed.), *Principles and Practice of Forensic Psychiatry*, p.198.

4 Ibid.

5 Ibid., p.18

6 Ibid., p.16.

7 Ibid., p.19.

8 Ibid., p.20.

9 Ibid., p.21.

10 Goldstein, R. L., and Rotter, M., 'The Psychiatrist's Guide to Right and Wrong: Judicial Standards of Wrongfulness since McNaughton', *Bulletin of the Academy of Psychiatry and the Law*, 16:4 (1988), pp.359–67.

11 Rosner (ed.), *Principles and Practice of Forensic Psychiatry*, p.19.

12 Ibid., p.199.

13 Applebaum and Gutheil, *Clinical Handbook*, p.279.

14 Ibid., p.277.

15 Tighe, J. A., 'Francis Wharton and the Nineteenth-Century Insanity Defense: The Origins of a Reform Tradition', *American Journal of Legal History*, 27 (1983), p.223.

16 'American Psychiatric Association Statement on the Insanity Defense', *American Journal of Psychiatry*, 140 (1983), p.6.

17 Al-Kāsānī (ʿAlā' al-Dīn Abū Bakr al-Ḥanafī), *Badā'iʿ al-Ṣanā'iʿ fī Tartīb al-Sharā'iʿ* (Beirut: Dār al-Kitāb al-ʿArabī, 1974), vol.7, p.233; al-Zaylāʿī (Fakhr al-Dīn ʿUthmān ibn ʿAlī), *Tabayyūn al-Ḥaqā'iq Sharḥ Kanz al-Daqā'iq* (Cairo: Maṭbaʿah Būlāq, 1315 AH), vol.7, p.98; al-Māwardī, *al-Aḥkām al-Sulṭāniyyah*, p.219; al-Sharbīnī, *Mughnī al-Muḥtāj*, vol.9, p.321.

18 ʿAwdah (ʿAbd al-Qādir), *al-Tashrīʿ al-Jinā'ī al-Islāmī* (Beirut: Dār al-Kitāb al-ʿArabī, n.d.), vol.2, p.6.

19 Al-Ḥaṭṭāb, *Mawāhib al-Jalīl*, vol.6, p.231; al-Ramlī (Shams al-Dīn Muḥammad ibn Aḥmad ibn al-Shihāb), *Nihāyah al-Muḥtāj ilā Sharḥ al-Minhāj* (Cairo: Maṭbaʿah Muṣṭafā al-Bābī al-Ḥalabī, 1386 AH), vol.6, p.235; al-Shāfiʿī, *al-Umm* (Cairo: Maṭbaʿah Būlāq, 1321 AH), vol.6, p.45; Ibn al-Nujaym (Zayn al-ʿĀbidīn ibn Ibrāhīm), *al-Baḥr al-Rā'iq Sharḥ Kanz al-Daqā'iq* (Beirut: Maṭbaʿah Dār al-Maʿārif, n.d.), vol.8, p.287; al-Sharbīnī, *Mughnī al-Muḥtāj*, vol.9, p.310.

20 Majmūʿah min al-ʿUlamā', *al-Mawsūʿah al-Fiqhiyyah* (Kuwait: Wazārah al-Awqāf wa al-Shu'ūn al-Islāmiyyah, 1989), vol.6, pp.99–110.

21 Ibid., p.99; Ibn al-Mandhir (Abū Bakr Muḥammad ibn Ibrāhīm), *al-Ijmāʿ* (Qaṭar: Maṭābiʿ al-Dawḥah, 1981) vol.10, pp.99–100; al-Nasafī (Abū al-Barakāt ʿAbd Allāh), *Kashf al-Asrār Sharḥ al-Muṣannif ʿalā al-Manār* (1st edn., Cairo: al-Maṭbaʿah al-Amīriyyah bi Būlāq, 1316 AH), vol.4, p.274.

22 ʿAwdah, *al-Tashrīʿ al-Jinā'ī*, vol.2, p.584.

23 Ibid.

24 Majmūʿah min al-ʿUlamā', *al-Mawsūʿah al-Fiqhiyyah*, pp.99–110.

25 Abū Zahrah (Muḥammad), *al-Wilāyah ʿalā al-Nafs* (Khartoum: al-Ḥalaqah al-Dirāsiyyah al-Rābiʿah li al-Buḥūth fī al-Qānūn, 1972), p.606.

26 Al-Jazīrī (ʿAbd al-Raḥmān), *al-Fiqh ʿalā al-Madhāhib al-Arbaʿah* (Cairo: Dār al-Rayyān li al-Turāth, 1987), vol.4, p.281.

NOTES TO CHAPTER 3

1 Burszatajn, H., et al., '*Parens Patriae* Consideration in Commitment Procedures', *Psychiatry Quarterly*, 59:3 (Fall

1988), pp.165–81.

2 Applebaum and Gutheil, *Clinical Handbook*, pp.133–44.

3 Stromberg, C. D., and Stone, A. A., 'A Model State Law on Civil Commitment of the Mentally Ill' in Rosner (ed.), *Principles and Practice of Forensic Psychiatry*, 1996), p.114.

4 Cleveland, S., Mulvey, E. P., Applebaum, P. S., et al., 'Do Dangerousness-Oriented Commitment Laws Restrict Hospitalization of Patients Who Need Treatment? A Test', *Hospital and Community Psychiatry*, 40 (1989), pp.266–71.

5 Hiday, V. A., et al., 'Interpreting the Effectiveness of Involuntory Outpatient Commitment: A Conceptual Model', *Journal of the American Academy of Psychiatry and Law*, 25:1 (1997), pp.5–15.

6 Al-Shaykh Mubārak, *al-Tadāwī wa al-Mas'ūliyyah al-Ṭibbiyyah*, p.196.

7 Al-Disūqī (Muḥammad ibn ʿUrfah al-Mālikī), *Ḥāshiyah al-Disūqī ʿalā al-Sharḥ al-Kabīr* (Cairo: Maṭbaʿah ʿĪsā al-Bābī al-Ḥalabī, n.d.), vol.4, p.355; Majmūʿah min ʿUlamā' al-Hind, *al-Fatāwā al-Hindiyyah* (Cairo: Maṭbaʿah Bulāq, 1310 AH) vol.4, p.499; Ibn al-Nujaym, *al-Ashbāh wa al-Naẓā'ir*, vol.8, p.33.

8 Ibn Qayyim al-Jawziyyah, *Iʿlām al-Muwaqqiʿīn ʿan Rabb al-ʿĀlamīn* (Beirut: Dār al-Fikr, 1397 AH), vol.2, p.22.

9 Ibn Ḥazm (al-Imām Abū Muḥammad ʿAlī al-Ẓāhirī), *al-Muḥallā Sharḥ al-Mujallā* (Cairo: al-Matābiʿ al-Munīriyyah, 1350 AH), vol.10, p.444.

10 Al-Shaykh Mubārak, *al-Tadāwī wa al-Mas'ūliyyah al-Ṭibbiyyah*, p.202.

11 Ibn Farḥūn, *Tabṣirah al-Ḥukkām*, vol.2, p.245; also, *al-Dībāj al-Mudhahhab fī Maʿrifah Aʿyān ʿUlamā' al-Madhhab* (1st edn., Beirut: Dār al-Kutub al-ʿIlmiyyah, n.d.), p.274.

12 Al-Qurṭubī, (Abu 'Abdullah al-Anṣari), *Al-Jāmiʿ li Aḥkām al-Qur'ān* (Beirut: Dār Iḥyā' al-Turāth al-ʿArabī, n.d.), pp.1–20.

13 Majmūʿah min ʿUlamā' al-Hind, *al-Fatāwā al-Hindiyyah*, vol.5, p.358; Ibn Qayyim al-Jawziyyah, *Iʿlām al-Muwaqqiʿīn*, vol.2, p.393.

14 Ibn Qāḍī Samāwah (Badr al-Dīn Maḥmūd ibn Isrā'īl), *Jāmiʿ al-Fuṣṣūlayn* (Cairo: al-Maṭbaʿah al-Azhariyyah, 1300 AH), vol.2, p.186; al-Shāfiʿī, *al-Umm*, vol.6, p.53.

15 Rosner (ed), *Principles and Practice of Forensic Psychiatry*, pp.122–125.

16 Abū Zahrah, *al-Wilāyah ʿalā al-Nafs*, p.606.

17 Majmūʿah min ʿUlamā' al-Hind, *al-Fatāwā al-Hindiyyah*, vol.5, p.358.

NOTES TO CHAPTER 4

1 Mullā Khusrū (Muḥammad ibn

Farāmūz), *Mir'at al-Uṣūl fī Sharḥ Mirqāt al Wūṣūl* (al-Astānah [Istanbul]: Maṭbaʿah Muḥammad Asʿad, 1300 AH), p.321.

2 Al-Jubūrī (Ḥusayn Khalaf), *ʿAwāriḍ al-Ahliyyah ʿinda al-ʿUsūliyyīn* (Makkah: al-Buhūth al-ʿIlmiyyah wa Iḥyā' al-Turāth al-Islāmī / Markaz Buhūth al-Dirāsāh al-Islāmiyyah, Jāmiʿah Umm al-Qurā, 1988), p.52.

3 Ibid., p.119.

4 Al-Namrī (Abū ʿUmar Yūsuf ibn ʿAbd Allāh), *Kitāb al-Kāfī* (1st edn., Riyadh: Maktabah al-Riyāḍ al-Ḥadīthah, 1978), vol.1, p.284; al-Sarakhsī (Muḥammad ibn Aḥmad ibn Abī Sahl), *al-Mabsūṭ* (1st edn., Cairo: Maṭbaʿah al-Saʿādah, 1320 AH), vol.2, p.162.

5 Amīr Bādshāh (Muḥammad Amīn), *Taysīr al-Taḥrīr* (Cairo: Maṭbaʿah Muṣṭafā al-Bābī al-Ḥalabī, 1350 AH), vol.2, p.419.

6 Al-Khuḍrī (al-Shaykh Muḥammad), *Uṣūl al-Fiqh* (5th edn., Cairo: al-Maktabah al-Tijāriyyah al-Kubrā, 1965), p.321.

7 Al-ʿAynī (ʿAbd al-Raḥmān ibn Abī Bakr), *Sharḥ al-Manār* (MS no. 3947, Baghdad: Maktabah al-Awqāf al-ʿĀmmah, n.d.), p.946.

8 *Mawsūʿah al-Ḥadīth al-Sharīf:* Abū Dāwūd, *Sunan Abu Dāwūd*, Bāb al-Ḥudūd, Hadith no.3822.)

9 Al-Ḥājj (Ibn Amīr), *al-Taqrīr wa al-Taḥbir* (1st edn., Cairo: al-Maṭbaʿah al-Amīriyyah bi Būlāq, 1314 AH), vol.2, p.174; Badrān (Badrān Abū al-ʿAynayn), *Al-Zawāj wa al-Ṭalāq fī al-Islām* (Alexandria: Mu'assassah Shabāb al-Jāmiʿah, n.d.), p.47.

10 Al-Rāzī (Muḥammad ibn Abī Bakr ibn ʿAbd al-Qādir), *Mukhtār al-Ṣiḥāḥ* (1st edn., Beirut: Dār al-Kitāb al-ʿArabī, 1967), p.412.

11 Al-ʿAynī, *Sharḥ al-Manār*, p.950.

12 Amīr Bādshāh, *Taysīr al-Taḥrīr*, vol.2, p.424.

13 Simon, *Clinical Psychiatry*, p.189.

14 Ibn ʿĀbidīn (Muḥammad Amīn ibn ʿUmar ibn ʿAbd al-ʿAzīz), *Ḥāshiyah Ibn ʿĀbidīn* (Cairo: Maṭbaʿah Muṣṭafā al-Bābī al-Ḥalabī, 1966), vol. 5, pp.415–425.

15 Ibn ʿAbd al-Salām, *Qawāʿid al-Aḥkām*, vol.2, p.125.

16 Al-Sanhūrī (ʿAbd al-Razzāq), *al-Wasīṭ fī Sharḥ al-Qānūn al-Madanī* (Cairo: Dār al-Nashr li al-Jāmiʿāt, 1956), vol.9, p.408.

17 Ibid., p.222.

18 Al-Qurṭubī (Abū ʿAbd Allāh Muḥammad al-Anṣārī), *al-Jāmiʿ li Aḥkām al-Qur'ān*, vol.5, p.38; Ibn al-Humām (Kamāl al-Dīn al-Wasīwāsī), *Sharḥ Fatḥ al-Qadīr ʿalā al-Hidāyah Sharḥ Bidāyah al-Mubtadī'* (Cairo: Maṭbaʿah Muṣṭafā Muḥammad, 1356 AH), vol.8, p.194.

19 Ibn Ḥazm, *al-Muḥallā Sharḥ al-Mujallā*, vol.8, p.286.

20 Al-Rāzī, *Mukhtār al-Siḥāḥ*, p.302; al-Jubūrī, *ʿAwāriḍ al-Ahliyyah*, p.137.

21 Al-Ḥājj, *al-Taqrīr wa al-Taḥbir*, vol.2, p.201; al-Anṣārī

(Muḥammad ibn Niẓām al-Dīn), *Fawātiḥ al-Raḥmūt Sharḥ Musallam al-Thabūt* (1st edn., Cairo: al-Maṭbaʿah al-Amīriyyah bi Bulāq, 1322 AH), vol.1, p.164.

22 Madkūr (Muḥammad ʿAbd al-Salām), *Mabāḥith al-Ḥukm ʿinda al-Uṣūliyīn.* (Cairo: Ṭabʿ Dār al-Nahḍah, n.d.), vol.1, p.301.

23 Al-Qurṭubī, *al-Jāmiʿ li Aḥkām al-Qur'ān*, vol.5, p.37.

24 Al-Jubūrī, *ʿAwāriḍ al-Ahliyyah*, p.138.

25 Al-Jazīrī, *al-Fiqh ʿalā al-Madhāhib al-Arbaʿah*, vol.1, pp.346–349.

26 Ibid.

27 Ibid.

28 Ibn Qudāmah (ʿAbd Allāh ibn Aḥmad al-Maqdisī), *al-Mughnī Sharḥ Mukhtaṣar al-Khiraqī* (Cairo: Maṭbaʿah al-Imām, 1965), vol.6, p.535; al-Sharbīnī, *Mughnī al-Muḥtāj*, vol.4, p.137; Ibn ʿĀbidīn, *Ḥāshiyah*, vol.5, p.342; al-Ḥaṭṭāb, *Mawāhib al-Jalīl*, vol.6, p.232; al-Zurqānī (ʿAbd al-Bāqī ibn Yūsuf), *Sharḥ al-Zurqānī ʿalā Mukhtaṣar al-Khalīl.* (Cairo: Maṭbaʿah Muḥammad Afandī Muṣṭafā, n.d.) vol.8, p.322.

29 Ibid.

30 Ibid.

NOTES TO CHAPTER 5

1 Badrān, *Al-Zawāj wa al-Ṭalāq*, p.443–45.

2 Ibid., 317.

3 Ibid., pp.312–313.

4 Ibid., pp.312–14.

5 Ibid., p.314; al-Jazīrī, *al-Fiqh ʿalā al-Madhāhib al-Arbaʿah*, vol.2, p.132.

6 Ibid.

7 Ibn Qayyim al-Jawziyyah, *Zād al-Maʿād fī Hadyi Khayr al-ʿIbād* (Cairo: Maṭbaʿah al-Bābī al-Ḥalabī, n.d.), vol.4, p.59.

8 Badrān, *Al-Zawāj wa al-Ṭalāq*, p.312.

9 Ibid.; al-Jazīrī, *al-Fiqh ʿalā al-Madhāhib al-Arbaʿah*, vol.3, p.406.

10 Ibid., vol.3, p.298.

NOTES TO CHAPTER 6

1 Al-Ṣanʿānī (Muḥammad ibn Ismāʿīl), *Subul al-Salām Sharḥ Bulūgh al-Marām* (Cairo: Maṭbaʿah al-Imām, n.d.), vol.3, p.226.

2 Al-Kāsānī (ʿAlā' al-Dīn), *Badā'iʿ al Ṣanā'iʿ*, vol.5, p.252.

3 Ibn Qayyim al-Jawziyyah, *Zād al-Maʿād*, vol.4, p.241.

4 Ṣāliḥ (Saʿd Ibrāhīm), *ʿAlāqat al-Ābā' bi al-Abnā' fī al-Sharīʿah al-Islāmiyyah: Dirāsah Fiqhiyyah Muqāranah* (Jeddah: Dār Tuhāmah li al-Nashr, 1981), pp.95–102.

5 Ibid.; see also, *Mawsūʿah al-Ḥadīth al-Sharīf:* Abū Dāwūd, *Sunan, Kitāb al-Ṭalāq*, no.1938.

6 Ṣāliḥ, *ʿAlāqat al-Ābā' bi al-Abnā'*, p.95.

7 Al-Ṣanʿānī, *Subul al-Salām*, vol.3, p.226; al-Shawkānī (Muḥammad ibn ʿAlī), *Nayl al-Awṭār (Sharḥ Muntahā al-Akhbār li ʿAbd al-Salām ibn Taymiyyah)* (Cairo:

Maṭbaʿah Muṣṭafā al-Bāb al-Ḥalabī, n.d.), vol.6, p.369.

8 Ibn al-Mundhir, *al-Ijmāʿ*, vol.4, p.8.

9 Al-Zaylāʿī, *Tabayyun al-Ḥaqā'iq*, vol.3, p.37.

10 Ibid., p.47.

11 Al-Bahūtī, *Kashshāf al-Qināʿ*, vol.2, p.326.

12 Al-Zaylāʿī, *Tabayyun al-Ḥaqā'iq*, vol.3, p.47.

13 Ibn Qudāmah, *al-Mughnī*, vol.9, p.297.

14 Al-Disūqī, *Ḥāshiyah*, vol.2, p.489.

15 Ibid.; Ṣāliḥ, *ʿAlāqat al-Ābā' bi al-Abnā'*, p.196.

16 Ibn Qayyim al-Jawziyyah, *Zād al-Maʿād*, vol.4, p.259.

17 Al-Zaylāʿī, *Tabayyun al-Ḥaqā'iq*, vol.3, p.46; Ibn ʿĀbidīn, *Ḥāshiyah*, vol.2, p.272.

18 Ibn Qayyim al-Jawziyyah, *Zād al-Maʿād*, vol.4, p.258; Ibn Qudāmah, *al-Mughnī*, vol.9, p.297.

19 Ṣāliḥ, *ʿAlāqat al-Ābā' bi al-Abnā'*, p.114–122.

20 Ibid.

21 Ibid.

22 Ibid.

23 Ibn Qudāmah, *al-Mughnī*, vol.9, p.306.

24 Al-Ramlī, *Nihāyat al-Muḥtāj*, vol.6, p.306; Al-Bahūtī, *Kashshāf al-Qināʿ*, vol.3, p.328.

25 Ibid., p.373.

26 Al-Jalabī, Qutaybah Sālim, (Chaleby, Kutaiba S.) *al-Ṭibb al-Nafsī wa al-Qaḍā'* (Cairo: Dār al-Anjlaw, 1994), p.170.

NOTES TO CHAPTER 7

1 Helfer, R. E., and Kempe, R. S., *The Battered Child* (4th edn., University of Chicago Press: Chicago, 1987), p.164.

2 Shields, N. M., McCall, G. J. and Hanneke, C. R., 'Patterns of Family and Non-family Violence', *Violence and Victims*, 3 (1988), pp.83–97.

3 Ibid.

4 Muḥammad (Muḥammad ʿAbd al-Jawād), *Ḥimāyah al-Ṭufūlah fī al-Sharīʿa al-Islāmiyyah wa al-Qānūn al-Duwalī al-ʿĀmm wa al-Sudānī* (Alexandria: Munsha'a al-Maʿārif, n.d.), p.31.

5 *Mawsūʿah al-Ḥadīth al-Sharīf*: Muslim, *Ṣaḥīḥ*, *Kitāb al-Birr wa al-ʿIlm wa al-Adāb*, no.4765.

6 Muḥammad, *Ḥimāyah al-Ṭufūlah*, p.36.

7 *Mawsūʿah al-Ḥadīth al-Sharīf*: al-Tirmidhī, *Sunan*, *Kitāb al-Ḥudūd*, no. 1344.

8 ʿUways (ʿAbd al-Ḥalīm), *al-Ḥudūd fī al-Sharīʿah al-Islāmiyyah* (Jeddah: Manshūrāt al-Sharq al-Awsaṭ, n.d.), p.39.

9 *Mawsūʿah al-Ḥadīth al-Sharīf*: al-Tirmidhī, *Kitāb al-Ḥudūd*, no. 1320.

10 *Mawsūʿah al-Ḥadīth al-Sharīf*: Ibn Mājah, *Sunan*, *Kitāb al-Tijārah*, no. 83; ʿUways, *al-Ḥudūd*, p.47.

11 Ibid.

12 Ibn Qudāmah, *al-Mughnī*, vol.9,

p.359; al-Jaṣṣās (Aḥmad ibn ʿAlī al-Rāzī), *Aḥkām al-Qur'ān al-Karīm* (Cairo: Maṭbaʿah al-Awqāf al-Islāmiyyah, Dār al-Khilāfah al-ʿIlmiyyah, 1335 AH), vol.1, p.144; al-Kāsānī, *Badā'iʿ al-Ṣanā'iʿ*, vol.10, p.479; al-Dardīr (Aḥmad ibn Muḥammad), *al-Sharḥ al-Ṣaghīr ilā Aqrab al-Masālik ilā Madhhab al-Imām Mālik*. (Cairo: Dār al-Maʿārif, 1984), vol.4, p.374.

13 Ṣāliḥ, *ʿAlāqat al-Ābā' bi al-Abnā'*, p.252.

14 Ibn Qudāmah, *al-Mughnī*, vol.7, p.667.

15 Abū Zahrah (al-Shaykh Muḥammad Aḥmad), *al-Jarīmah wa al-ʿUqūbah fī al-Fiqh al-Islāmī* (Cairo: Dār al-Fikr al-ʿArabī, n. d.), p.474.

16 Ṣāliḥ, *ʿAlāqat al-Ābā' bi l-Abnā'*, p.252.

17 Al-Qurṭubī, *al-Jāmiʿ li Aḥkām al-Qur'ān*, vol.1, p.627; al-Sharbīnī, *Mughnī*, vol.1, p.18; Ibn Ḥazm, *al-Muḥallā*, vol.8, p.334.

18 Ibn Mājah, *Sunan Ibn Mājah*, (Cairo: Maṭbaʿah Muṣṭafā al-Bābī al-Ḥalabi, 1953), vol.2, p.895.

19 Al-Qurṭubī, *al-Jāmiʿ li Aḥkām al-Qur'ān*, vol.1, p.627.

20 Al-Aṣbaḥī, *al-Mudawwanah*, vol.6, p.106.

21 *Mawsūʿah al-Ḥadīth al-Sharīf*: Ibn Ḥanbal, *Musnad*, hadith no. 94, 141.

22 Dobson, J., *Raising Children* (Wheaton, Ill.: Tyndale House Publishing, 1982), pp.74–92.

23 Al-Ghazālī (Abū Ḥāmid Muḥammad al-Ṭūsī), *Iḥyā' ʿUlūm al-Dīn* (Cairo: Maṭbaʿah Muṣṭafā al-Bābī al-Ḥalabī, 1939), vol.2, p.83; *Mawsūʿah al-Ḥadīth al-Sharīf*: Ibn Ḥanbal, *Musnad*, Hadith no. 6467.

24 Al-Kāsānī, *Badā'iʿ al-Ṣanā'iʿ*, vol.10, p.779

25 Abū Zahrah, *al-Jarīmah wa al-ʿUqūbah*, p.480.

26 Ibid.

27 Al-Ramlī, *Nihāyah al-Muḥtāj*, vol.6, p.273; Ibn Qudāmah, *al-Mughnī*, vol.9, p.296; Ibn Qayyim al-Jawziyyah, *Zād al-Maʿād*, vol.4, p.259.

28 Ibid.; Ṣāliḥ, *ʿAlāqat al-Ābā' bi al-Abnā'*, p.106.

29 Kattan, H., "Child Abuse in Saudi Arabia: Report on Ten Cases", *Annals of Saudi Medicine*, 1994, vol. 14, pp.129–133.

30 Al-Dasūqī, *Ḥāshiyah*, vol.2, p.48; al-Ramlī, *Nihāyah al-Muḥtāj*, vol.6, p.273; Ibn Qudāmah, *al-Mughnī*, vol.9, p.296.

31 This opinion was expressed in a presentation at the first symposium on 'Psychiatry and Jurisprudence', held in 1990, Ṭa'if, Saudi Arabia.

32 Hāshim, *al-Qaḍā' wa Niẓām al-Ithbāt*, p.327.

33 Al-Disūqī, *Ḥāshiyah*, vol.12, p.46.

34 Ibn Qayyim al-Jawziyyah, *Iʿlām al-Muwaqqiʿīn*, vol.1, p.111.

35 Al-Qurṭubī, *al-Jāmiʿ li Aḥkām al-Qur'ān*, vol.3, p.1980 (n.d.)

36 Ṣāliḥ, *ʿAlāqat al-Ābā' bi al-Abnā'*, p.213; Al-Disūqī, *Ḥāshiyah*, vol.12, p.66.

NOTES TO CHAPTER 8

1 Al-Anṭākī, *Tadhkhirah Ūlī al-Albāb*, vol.1, p.9.

2 Al-Aṣbaḥī, *al-Mudawwanah*, vol.4, p.374.

3 Al-Bahūtī, *Kashshāf al-Qināʿ*, vol.6, p.10; Ibn Ḍawyān (Ibrāhīm ibn Sālim), *Manār al-Sabīl fī Sharḥ al-Dalīl* (1st edn., Damascus: al-Maṭbaʿah al-Hāshimiyyah, 1958), vol.2, p.337.

4 Al-Sharbīnī, *Mughnī*, vol.4, p.309.

5 Al-Shaykh Mubārak, *al-Tadāwī wa al-Mas'ūliyyah al-Ṭibbiyyah*, p.30.

6 Al-Haytamī (Ibn Ḥajar Abū al-ʿAbbās Aḥmad ibn Shihāb al-Dīn), *Fatḥ al-Jawād Sharḥ al-Irshād ʿalā Matn al-Irshād li Sharaf al-Dīn al-Maqrī* (2nd edn., Cairo: Maṭbaʿah al-Bābī al-Ḥalabī, 1971), vol.2, p.58.

7 Al-Nawawī, *Rawḍat al-Ṭālibīn*, vol.10, p.179.

8 Al-Shāfiʿī, *al-Risālah*, vol.6, p.52.

9 Al-Shaykh Mubārak, *al-Tadāwī wa al-Mas'ūliyyah al-Ṭibbiyyah*, p.154.

10 Ibn Qayyim al-Jawziyyah, *Iʿlām al-Muwaqqiʿīn*, vol.2, p.152.

11 Al-Ḥaṣkafī (Muḥammad ʿAlā' al-Dīn), *al-Durr al-Muhktār Sharḥ Tanwīr al-Abṣār* (Cairo: Maṭbaʿah Muṣṭafā al-Bābī al-Ḥalabī, 1966) vol.6, p.69.

12 Majmūʿah min ʿUlamā' al-Hind, *al-Fatāwā al-Hindiyyah*, vol.6, p.34.

13 Mālik ibn Anas, *al-Muwaṭṭā* (rescension of Yaḥyā ibn Yaḥyā al-Laythī) (Beirut: Dār al-Nafā'is, n.d.), p.614.

14 Ibn al-Ikhwah (Muḥammad ibn Muḥammad al-Qurashī), *Maʿālim al-Qurbah fī Aḥkām al-Ḥisbah* (London: Luzac & Co., 1937), p.164.

15 Ibn Mufliḥ (Abū ʿAbd Allāh ibn Aḥmad al-Tilmisānī), *al-Furūʿ*. (1st edn., Cairo: al-Maṭbaʿah al-Miṣriyyah, 1932), vol.2, p.274; al-Baʿlī (Aḥmad ibn ʿAbd Allāh), *al-Rawḍ al-Nadī Sharḥ Kāfī al-Mubtadī* (Cairo: al-Maṭbaʿah al-Salafiyyah, n.d.), p.217.

16 Ibn Farḥūn, *al-Dībāj*, pp.141, 159; Ibn al-ʿImād (Abū al-Falāḥ al-Ḥanbalī), *Shadharāt al-Dhahab fī Akhbār man Dhahab* (2nd edn., Beirut: Dār al-Masīrah, 1979), vol.3, p.223; Ibn Khallikān (Abū al-ʿAbbās Shams al-Dīn), *Wafiyāt al-Aʿyān wa Anbā' wa Abnā' al-Zamān* (Beirut: al-Thaqāfah, 1972), vol.4, p.219 and vol3, p.61; Ibn Farḥūn, *Tabṣirah al-Ḥukkām*, vol.2, p.243.

17 Ibn Rushd (Muḥammad ibn Aḥmad ibn Muḥammad al-Qurṭubī), *Bidāyah al-Mujtahid wa Nihāyah al-Muqtaṣid* (Damascus: Dār al-Fikr, n.d.), vol.2, p.313.

18 Al-Shāfiʿī, *al-Umm*, vol.7, p.166.

19 Qā'id (Usāmah ᶜAbd Allāh), *al-Mas'ūliyah al-Jinā'iyyah li al-Aṭibbā': Dirāsah Muqārinah fī al-Sharīᶜah al-Islāmiyyah wa al-Qānūn al-Waḍᶜī* (Cairo: Dār al-Nahḍah al-ᶜArabiyyah, 1987), p.195.

20 Ibn al-Shaḥnah (Abū al-Walīd Ibrahim), *Lisān al-Ḥukkām fī Maᶜarifah al-Aḥkām* (2nd edn., Cairo: Maṭbaᶜah al-Bābī al-Ḥalabī, 1973), p.292.

21 Al-Ṭarābulsī (ᶜAlā' al-Dīn Abū al-Ḥasan ᶜAlī ibn Khalīl al-Ḥanafī), *Muᶜīn al-Ḥukkām fi-mā Yataradad bayn al-Khaṣmayn min al-Aḥkām* (2nd edn., Cairo: Maṭbaᶜah Muṣṭafā al-Bābī al-Ḥalabī, 1973), p.204.

22 Al-Ghazālī, *Iḥyā'*, vol.2, p.216; Ibn al-Munāṣif (Muḥammad ibn ᶜĪsā ibn Muḥammad), *Tanbīh al-Ḥukkām ᶜalā Ma'ākhidh al-Aḥkām* (Tunis: al-Maṭābiᶜa al-Muwaḥḥadah, Dār al-Turkī, 1988), p.354.

23 Ibn Qudāmah, *al-Mughnī*, vol.5, p.538; Ibn Mufliḥ, *al-Furūᶜ*, vol.2, p.453.

24 Ibn Qayyim al-Jawziyyah, *al-Ṭibb al-Nabawī* (ed.) ᶜAbd al-Ghanī ᶜAbd al-Khāliq (Cairo: Maṭbaᶜah al-ᶜĪsā al-Bābī al-Ḥalabī, n.d.), p.130.

25 Al-Zarkashī, *al-Manthūr*, vol.2, p.176.

26 Ibn Qāḍī Samāwah, *Jāmiᶜ al-Fuṣṣūlayn*, vol.2, p.116; Ibn al-Bazzāz (al-Shaykh Ḥāfiẓ al-Dīn Muḥammad ibn al-Shihāb), *al-Fatāwā al-Bazzāziyyah wa al-Jāmiᶜ al-Wajīz* (in the margins of vols.4–6, *al-Fatāwā al-Hindīyyah*, vol.6, p.408; vol.5, p.150; al-Baghdādī (Ghiyāth al-Dīn Abū Aḥmad), *Mujmaᶜ al-Ḍamānāt* (Cairo: al-Maṭbaᶜah al-Khayriyyah, 1308 AH), p.173; al-Maqrī (Abū ᶜAbd Allāh al-Tilmisānī), *al-Qawāᶜid* (Makkah: Sharikah Makkah li al-Ṭibāᶜah wa al-Nashr, n.d.) vol.2, p.611.

27 Al-Wanshirīsī, *al-Miᶜyār al-Muᶜrib*, vol.8, p.325; al-Ḥaṭṭāb, *Mawāhib al-Jalīl*, vol.1, p.33; al-Disūqī, *Ḥāshiyah*, vol.3, p.451; al-Maqrī, *al-Qawāᶜid*, vol.2, p.611.

28 Al-Zarkashī, *al-Manthūr*, vol.1, p.135; Ibn al-Nujaym, *al-Ashbāh wa al-Naẓā'ir*, p.162; Ibn Mufliḥ, *al-Furūᶜ*, vol.2, p.474; Ibn Qayyim al-Jawziyyah, *Iᶜlām al-Muwaqqiᶜīn*, vol.4, p.223.

29 Ibn Ḥazm, *al-Muḥallā*, vol.10, p.471; al-Ḥaṭṭāb, *Mawāhib al-Jalīl*, vol.6, p.235.

30 Al-Ṭaḥṭāwī, *Ḥāshiyah*, vol4, p.226; al-Baghdādī, *Majmaᶜ al-Ḍamānāt*, p.160; al-Ḥaṭṭāb, *Mawāhib al-Jalīl*, vol.6, p.235.

31 Al-Mirdādī (al-Shaykh ᶜAlā' al-Dīn ᶜAlī al-Ḥanbalī), *al-Inṣāf fī Maᶜarifah al-Rājiḥ min al-Khilāf ᶜalā Madhhab al-Imām Aḥmad ibn Ḥanbal* (Beirut: Dār Iḥyā' al-Turāth al-ᶜArabī, 1968), vol.9, p.455; Ibn Mufliḥ, *al-Furūᶜ*, vol.5, p.633.

32 Al-Nawawī, *Rawḍat al-Ṭālibīn*,

vol.9, p.138; al-Zarkashī, *al-Manthūr*, vol.2, p.176.

APPENDIX

1 Al-Leḥaidān, Shaykh Ṣāliḥ, *Ḥāl al-Muttaham fī Majlis al-Qaḍā'* (Riyadh: Masafi li al-Ṭab[c], 1985).

BIBLIOGRAPHY

ARABIC WORKS

(In the alphabetical sorting of the Arabic names in this list the letter *ʿayn* and the definite article *al-* are ignored).

Abū Zahrah, al-Shaykh Muḥammad Aḥmad, *al-Jarīmah wa al-ʿUqūbah fī al-Fiqh al-Islāmī*. Cairo: Dār al-Fikr al-ʿArabī, n. d.

——*al-Wilāyah ʿalā al-Nafs*. Khartoum: al-Ḥalaqah al-Dirāsiyyah al-Rābiʿah li al-Buḥūth fī al-Qānūn. 1972.

Amīr Bādshāh (d. 972 AH/1565 CE), Muḥammad Amīn, *Taysīr al-Taḥrīr*. Cairo: Maṭbaʿah Muṣṭafā al-Bābī al-Ḥalabī, 1350 AH.

al-Anṣārī (d. 125 AH, Damascus), Muḥammad ibn Niẓām al-Dīn, *Fawātiḥ al-Raḥmūt Sharḥ Musallam al-Thabūt*. 1st edn. Cairo: al-Maṭbaʿah al-Amīriyyah bi Bulāq, 1322 AH.

al-Anṭākī (d. 1008 AH / 1600 CE, Cairo, Egypt), Dāwūd ibn ʿUmar al-Baṣīr, *Tadhkhirah Ūlī al-Albāb wa al-Jāmiʿ li al-ʿAjab al-ʿUjāb*. Cairo: Maṭbaʿah Muṣṭafā al-Bābī al-Ḥalabī, 1951. 2 vols.

al-Aṣbaḥī (d. 169 AH/795 CE, Madina), Mālik ibn Anas, *al-Mudawwanah al-Kubrā*. (Rescension of Saḥnūn). Cairo: Dār al-Fikr li al-Ṭibāʿah wa al-Nashr wa al-Tawzīʿ, 1978.

ʿAwdah, ʿAbd al-Qādir, *al-Tashrīʿ al-Jināʾī al-Islāmī*. Beirut: Dār al-Kitāb al-ʿArabī, n.d. 2 vols.

al-ʿAynī (d. 893 AH / 1488 CE, Damascus), ʿAbd al-Raḥmān ibn Abī Bakr, *Sharḥ al-Manār*. (MS no. 3947). Baghdad: Maktabah al-Awqāf al-ʿĀmmah, n.d.

al-Baʿlī (d. 1189 AH / 1775 CE, Damascus), Aḥmad ibn ʿAbd Allāh, *al-Rawḍ al-Nadī Sharḥ Kāfī al-Mubtadī*. Cairo: al-Maṭbaʿah al-Salafiyyah, n.d.

Badrān, Badrān Abū al-ʿAynayn. *Al-Zawāj wa al-Ṭalāq fī al-Islām*. Alexandria: Muʾassassah Shabāb al-Jāmiʿah, n.d.

al-Baghdādī (d. 618 AH / 1027 CE), Ghiyāth al-Dīn Abū Aḥmad, *Mujmaʿ al-Ḍamānāt*. Cairo: al-Maṭbaʿah al-Khayriyyah, 1308 AH.

al-Bahūtī (d. 1310 AH / 1892 CE, Cairo), Abū ʿAbd Allāh Muḥammad, *Kashshāf al-Qināʿ ʿalā Matn al-Iqnāʿ*. (Margins: *Sharḥ al-Zarqānī*). Cairo: Muḥammad Afandī Muṣṭafā, n.d.

al-Bukhārī (b. 194 AH, Bukhara), Muḥammad ibn Ismāʿīl. *Ṣaḥīḥ al-Bukhārī bi Sharḥ Fatḥ al-Bārī*. Cairo: al-Maṭbaʿah al-Khayriyyah, 1951. 13 vols.

Chaleby, Kutaiba: *see* Jalabī.

al-Dardīr (d. 1201 AH / 1786 CE, Cairo), Aḥmad ibn Muḥammad, *al-Sharḥ al-Ṣaghīr ilā Aqrab al-Masālik ilā Madhhab al-Imām Mālik*. (Margins: *Ḥāshiyyah al-Ṣāwī*). Cairo: Dār al-Maʿārif, 1984.

al-Disūqī (b. 1230 AH / 1815 CE, Cairo), Muḥammad ibn ʿUrfah al-Mālikī, *Ḥāshiyah al-Disūqī ʿalā al-Sharḥ al-Kabīr*. Cairo: Maṭbaʿah ʿĪsā al-Bābī al-Ḥalabī, n.d. 4 vols.

al-Ghazālī (b. 505 AH / 1111 CE, Khurasan), Abū Ḥāmid Muḥammad al-Ṭūsī, *Iḥyāʾ ʿUlūm al-Dīn*. Cairo: Maṭbaʿah al-Bābī al-Ḥalabī, 1939. 5 vols.

al-Ḥājj (b. 879 AH / 1474 CE, Aleppo, Syria), Ibn Amīr, *al-Taqrīr wa al-Taḥbīr*. 1st edn. Cairo: al-Maṭbaʿah al-Amīriyyah bi Būlāq, 1317 AH.

Hāshim, Muḥammad Maḥmūd, *al-Qaḍāʾ wa Niẓām al-Ithbāt fī al-Fiqh al-Islāmī wa al-Anẓimah al-Waḍʿiyyah*. Riyadh: ʿImādah Shuʾūn al-Maktabāt Jāmiʿah al-Malik Saʿūd, 1988.

al-Ḥaṣkafī (b. 1088 AH / 1677 CE, Damascus), Muḥammad ʿAlāʾ al-Dīn, *al-Durr al-Mukhtār Sharḥ Tanwīr al-Abṣār*. Cairo: Maṭbaʿah Muṣṭafā al-Bābī al-Ḥalabī, 1966. 8 vols.

al-Ḥaṭṭāb (b. 954 AH / 1547 CE, Morocco), Abū ʿAbd Allāh Muḥammad al-Ruʿaynī, *Mawāhib al-Jalīl li Sharḥ Mukhtaṣar al-Khalīl*. (Margins: *al-Tāj wa al-Iklīl*). Cairo: Maṭbaʿah al-Saʿādah, 1328 AH. 6 vols.

al-Haytamī (b. 947 AH / 1567 CE, Cairo), Ibn Ḥajar Abū al-ʿAbbās Aḥmad ibn Shihāb al-Dīn, *Fatḥ al-Jawād Sharḥ al-Irshād ʿalā Matn al-Irshād li Sharaf al-Dīn al-Maqrī*. 2nd edn. Cairo: Maṭbaʿah al-Bābī al-Ḥalabī, 1971.

al-Haytamī, Ibn Ḥajar Abū al-ʿAbbās Aḥmad ibn Shihāb al-Dīn, *al-Zawājir ʿan Iqtirāf al-Kabāʾir*. Beirut: Dār al-Maʿrifah, 1987.

Ibn ʿAbd al-Salām (9th century author), Abū Muḥammad ibn ʿAbd al-ʿAzīz al-Shāfiʿī, *Qawāʿid al-Aḥkām fī Maṣāliḥ al-'Anām*. Cairo: Dār al-Sharq li al-Ṭībāʿah, 1388 AH.

Ibn ʿĀbidīn (b. 837 AH / 1784 CE), Muḥammad Amīn ibn ʿUmar ibn ʿAbd al-ʿAzīz, *Ḥāshiyah Ibn ʿĀbidīn (Radd al-Muḥtār ʿalā Durr al-Mukhtār Sharḥ Tanwīr al-Abṣār)*. Cairo: Maṭbaʿah Muṣṭafā al-Bābī al-Ḥalabī, 1966. 8 vols.

Ibn al-Bazzāz (19th century author), al-Shaykh Ḥāfiẓ al-Dīn Muḥammad ibn al-Shihāb, *al-Fatāwā al-Bazzāziyyah wa al-Jāmiʿ al-Wajīz* in the margins of *al-Fatāwā al-Hindiyyah*, vols. 4–6. Cairo: Maṭbaʿah Būlāq, 1988.

Ibn Ḍawyān, Ibrāhīm ibn Sālim, *Manār al-Sabīl fī Sharḥ al-Dalīl*. 1st edn. Damascus: al-Maṭbaʿah al-Hāshimiyyah, 1958.

Ibn Farḥūn (b. 799 AH / 1397 CE, Madina), Ibrāhīm ibn ʿAlī al-Yaʿmurī, *al-Dībāj al-Mudhahhab fī Maʿrifah Aʿyān ʿUlamā' al-Madhhab*. 1st edn. Beirut: Dār al-Kutub al-ʿIlmiyyah, n.d.

——*Tabṣirah al-Ḥukkām fī Uṣūl al-Aqḍiyah wa Manāhij al-Aḥkām*. 1st edn. Cairo: al-Maṭbaʿah al-ʿĀmirah al-Sharafiyyah, 1301 AH.

Ibn Ḥanbal (author, 3rd century AH / 9th century CE), al-Imām Aḥmad Abū ʿAbd Allāh, *Musnad al-Imām Aḥmad* (In the margin of *Muntakhab Kanz al-ʿUmmāl fī Sunan al-Aqwāl wa al-Afʿāl*). Cairo: al-Maṭbaʿah al- Maymaniyyah, 1313 AH. 2 vols.

Ibn Ḥazm (b. 456 AH / 1064 CE, Spain), al-Imām Abū Muḥammad ʿAlī al-Ẓāhirī, *al-Muḥallā Sharḥ al-Mujallā*. Cairo: al-Matābiʿ al-Munīriyyah, 1350 AH. 12 vols.

Ibn al-Humām (b. 861 AH / 1457 CE, Egypt), Kamāl al-Dīn al-Wasīwāsī, *Sharḥ Fatḥ al-Qadīr ʿalā al-Hidāyah Sharḥ Bidāyah al-Mubtadī'*. Cairo: Maṭbaʿah Muṣṭafā Muḥammad, 1356 AH.

Ibn al-Ikhwah (b. 729 AH / 1329 CE), Muḥammad ibn Muḥammad al-Qurashī, *Maʿālim al-Qurbah fī Aḥkām al-Ḥisbah*. (copied and corrected by Reuben Levi) London: Luzac & Co., 1937.

Ibn al-ʿImād (b. 1089 AH / 1679 CE, Damascus), Abū al-Falāḥ al-Ḥanbalī, *Shadharāt al-Dhahab fī Akhbār man Dhahab*. 2nd edn. Beirut: Dār al-Masīrah, 1979.

Ibn Khallikān (b. 681 AH / 1282 CE, Iraq), Abū al-ʿAbbās Shams al-Dīn, *Wafiyāt al-Aʿyān wa Anbā' wa Abnā' al-Zamān*. (Ed. Iḥsān ʿAbbās). Beirut:

al-Thaqāfah, 1972. 8 vols.

Ibn Mājah (b. 273 AH / 887 CE, Qazwin), Muḥammad ibn Yazīd al-Qazwīnī Abū ʿAbd Allāh, *Sunan Ibn Mājah*. Cairo: Maṭbaʿah al-Ḥalabī, 1953.

Ibn Manẓūr (b. 630 AH, Baghdad), Jamāl al-Dīn Abū al-Faḍl, *Lisān al-ʿArab*. Beirut: Dār al-Lisān al-ʿArabī, n.d.

Ibn Mufliḥ (b. 1011 AH / 1603 CE, Damascus), Abū ʿAbd Allāh al-Maqdisī, *al-Ādāb al-Sharʿīyyah wa al-Minaḥ al-Marʿīyyah*. Riyadh: Maktabah al-Riyāḍ al-Ḥadīthah, 1391 AH.

Ibn Mufliḥ (b. 771 AH / 1370 CE, Morocco), Abū ʿAbd Allāh ibn Aḥmad al-Tilmisānī, *al-Furūʿ*. (Ed. and critique Aḥmad ibn ʿAbd Allāh ibn Ḥumaydān. 1st edn. Cairo: al-Maṭbaʿah al-Miṣriyyah, 1932.

Ibn al-Munāṣif (b. 620 AH / 1223 CE, Spain), Muḥammad ibn ʿĪsā ibn Muḥammad, *Tanbīh al-Ḥukkām ʿalā Maʾākhidh al-Aḥkām*. (Prepared for publication by ʿAbd al-Ḥafīẓ Manṣūr). Tunis: al-Maṭābiʿa al-Muwaḥḥadah, Dār al-Turkī, 1988.

Ibn al-Mandhir (d. 742 AH / 1340 CE), Abū Bakr Muḥammad ibn Ibrāhīm, *al-Ijmāʿ*. Qaṭar: Maṭābiʿ al-Dawḥah, 1981.

Ibn al-Nujaym (b. 970 AH / 1563 CE, Cairo), Zayn al-ʿĀbidīn ibn Ibrāhīm, *al-Baḥr al-Rāʾiq Sharḥ Kanz al-Daqāʾiq*. (With the completion of it by al-Ṭurī). Beirut: Maṭbaʿah Dār al-Maʿārif, n.d. 7 vols.

—— *al-Ashbāh wa al-Naẓāʾir*. Beirut: Dār al-Kutub al-ʿIlmiyyah, 1980.

Ibn Qāḍī Samāwah (b. 823 AH / 1420 CE, Turkey), Badr al-Dīn Maḥmūd ibn Isrāʾīl, *Jāmiʿ al-Fuṣṣūlayn* (In its margin *Jāmiʿ Aḥkām al-Ṣighār* of al-Astrūshīnī). 1st edn. Cairo: al-Maṭbaʿah al-Azhariyyah, 1300 AH.

Ibn Qāsim, ʿAbd al-Raḥmān ibn Muḥammad al-ʿĀṣimī, *Ḥāshiyah Ibn Qāsim ʿalā al-Rawḍ al-Murabbaʿ*. Cairo: al-ʿArabī Publishing, n.d. 7 vols.

Ibn Qayyim al-Jawziyyah (b. 769 AH / 1367 CE, Damascus), Shams al-Dīn Muḥammad ibn Abī Bakr al-Dimashqī, *Iʿlām al-Muwaqqiʿīn ʿan Rabb al-ʿĀlamīn*. Beirut: Dār al-Fikr, 1397 AH. 4 vols.

——*al-Ṭibb al-Nabawī*. (Ed. ʿAbd al-Ghanī ʿAbd al-Khāliq). Cairo: Maṭbaʿah al-ʿĪsā al-Bābī al-Ḥalabī, n.d.

——*al-Ṭuruq al-Ḥikmiyyah fī al-Siyāsah al-Sharʿiyyah*. (Ed. Dr. Muḥammad

Jamīl Ghāzī). Cairo: Maṭbaᶜah al-Madanī, n.d.

——*Zād al-Maᶜād fī Hadyi Khayr al-ᶜIbād*. Cairo: Maṭbaᶜah al-Bābī al-Ḥalabī, n.d. 4 vols.

Ibn Qudāmah (b. 620 AH / 1223 CE, Damascus), ᶜAbd Allāh ibn Aḥmad al-Maqdisī, *al-Mughnī Sharḥ Mukhtaṣar al-Khiraqī*. Cairo: Maṭbaᶜah al-Imām, 1965.

Ibn Rushd (b. 519 AH / 1125 CE, Spain), Muḥammad ibn Aḥmad ibn Muḥammad al-Qurṭubī, *Bidāyah al-Mujtahid wa Nihāyah al-Muqtaṣid*. Damascus: Dār al-Fikr, n.d.

Ibn al-Shaḥnah (b. 898 AH / 1412 CE, Syria), Abū al-Walīd Ibrahim, *Lisān al-Ḥukkām fī Maᶜarifah al-Aḥkām* (in Ṭarābulsī's book, *Muᶜīn al-Ḥukām)*. 2nd edn. Cairo: Maṭbaᶜah al-Bābī al-Ḥalabī, 1973.

al-Jalabī (contemporary), Qutaybah Sālim (Chaleby, Kotaiba), *al-Ṭibb al-Nafsī wa al-Qaḍā'*. Cairo: Dār al-Anjlaw, 1994.

al-Jaṣṣāṣ (d. 370 AH / 980 CE, Baghdad), Aḥmad ibn ᶜAlī al-Rāzī, *Aḥkām al-Qur'ān al-Karīm*. Cairo: Maṭbaᶜah al-Awqāf al-Islāmiyyah, Dār al-Khilāfah al-ᶜIlmiyyah, 1335 AH.

al-Jazīrī, ᶜAbd al-Raḥmān, *al-Fiqh ᶜalā al-Madhāhib al-Arbaᶜah*. Cairo: Dār al-Rayyān li al-Turāth, 1987.

al-Jubūrī, Ḥusayn Khalaf, *ᶜAwāriḍ al-Ahliyyah ᶜinda al-ᶜUsūliyyīn*. Makkah: al-Buhūth al-ᶜIlmiyyah wa Iḥyā' al-Turāth al-Islāmī, Jāmiᶜah Umm al-Qurā, 1988.

al-Kāsānī (d. 587 AH / 1191 CE, Syria), ᶜAlā' al-Dīn Abū Bakr al-Ḥanafī, *Badā'iᶜ al-Ṣanā'iᶜ fī Tartīb al-Sharā'iᶜ*. Beirut: Dār al-Kitāb al-ᶜArabī, 1974.

al-Khuḍrī (d. 1287 AH / 1870 CE, Cairo), al-Shaykh Muḥammad, *Uṣūl al-Fiqh*. 5th edn. Cairo: al-Maktabah al-Tijāriyyah al-Kubrā, 1965.

Al-Leḥaidān, Shaykh Ṣalīḥ, *Ḥāl al-Muttaham fī Majlis al-Qaḍā'*. Riyadh: Masafi li al-Ṭabᶜ, 1985.

Madkūr, Muḥammad ᶜAbd al-Salām, *Mabāḥith al-Ḥukm ᶜinda al-Uṣūliyīn*. Cairo: Ṭabᶜ Dār al-Nahḍah, n.d.

Majmūᶜah min al-ᶜUlamā', *al-Mawsūᶜah al-Fiqhiyyah*. Kuwait: Wazārah al-Awqāf wa al-Sha'ūn al-Islāmiyyah, 1989.

Majmūᶜah min ᶜUlamā' al-Hind, *al-Fatāwā al-Hindiyyah*. Cairo: Maṭbaᶜah

Bulāq, 1310 AH. 2 vols.

Mālik ibn Anas (3rd century AH / 9th century CE), *al-Muwaṭṭā*. (Rescension of Yaḥyā ibn Yaḥyā al-Laythī; prepared by Aḥmad Rātib ᶜArmūsh). Beirut: Dār al-Nafā'is, n.d.

al-Maqrī, Abū ᶜAbd Allāh al-Tilmisānī, *al-Qawāᶜid*. (Ed. and critique Aḥmad ibn ᶜAbd Allāh ibn Ḥumayd). Makkah: Sharikah Makkah li al-Ṭibāᶜah wa al-Nashr, n.d.

al-Māwardī (b. 450 AH/1058 CE, Basra, Iraq), Abū al-Ḥasan ᶜAlī ibn Muḥammad al-Baṣrī, *al-Aḥkām al-Sulṭāniyyah*. Beirut: Dār al-Kutub al-ᶜIlmiyyah, 1982.

Mawsūᶜah al-Ḥadīth al-Sharīf. CD ROM, 1st issue, Kuwait: Sharikah Ṣakhar li al-Ḥāsib al-Ālī, 1996.

al-Mirdādī (b. 885 AH / 1480 CE, Damascus), al-Shaykh ᶜAlā' al-Dīn ᶜAlī al-Ḥanbalī, *al-Inṣāf fī Maᶜarifah al-Rājiḥ min al-Khilāf ᶜalā Madhhab al-Imām Aḥmad ibn Ḥanbal*. Beirut: Dār Iḥyā' al-Turāth al-ᶜArabī, 1968.

Muḥammad, Muḥammad ᶜAbd al-Jawād. *Ḥimāyah al-Ṭufūlah fī al-Sharīᶜah al-Islāmiyyah wa al-Qānūn al-Duwalī al-ᶜĀmm wa al-Sudānī*. Alexandria: Munsha'a al-Maᶜārif, n.d.

Mullā Khusrū (b. 885 AH/1480 CE, Turkey), Muḥammad ibn Farāmūz, *Mir'at al-Uṣūl fī Sharḥ Mirqāt al Wūṣūl*. Al-Astānah [Istanbul]: Maṭbaᶜah Muḥammad Asᶜad, 1300 AH.

al-Namrī (d. 463 AH / 1071 CE, Spain), Abū ᶜUmar Yūsuf ibn ᶜAbd Allāh, *Kitāb al-Kāfī*. 1st edn. Riyadh: Maktabah al-Riyāḍ al-Ḥadīthah, 1978.

al-Nasafī (b. 710 AH / 1310 CE, Iṣfahan), Abū al-Barakāt ᶜAbd Allāh, *Kashf al-Asrār Sharḥ al-Muṣannif ᶜalā al-Manār*. 1st edn. Cairo: al-Maṭbaᶜah al-Amīriyyah bi Būlāq, 1316 AH.

al-Nawawī (b. 676 AH / 1277 CE, Syria), Abū Zakariyyā Yaḥyā al-Shāfiᶜī, *Sharḥ Ṣaḥīḥ Muslim*. 1st edn. Cairo: al-Maṭbaᶜah al-Miṣriyyah, 1346 AH.

——*Rawḍat al-Ṭālibīn*. Damascus: Maṭbaᶜah al-Maktab al-Islāmī li al-Ṭibāᶜah wa al-Nashr, n.d. 10 vols.

Qā'id, Usāmah ᶜAbd Allāh, *al-Mas'ūliyah al-Jinā'iyyah li al-Aṭibbā': Dirāsah Muqārinah fī al-Shariᶜah al-Islāmiyyah wa al-Qānūn al-Waḍᶜī*. Cairo: Dār al-Nahda al-ᶜArabiyyah, 1987.

al-Qalyūbī (b. 1069 AH / 1659 CE, Cairo), Shihāb al-Dīn Aḥmad, *Ḥāshīyatān ᶜalā*

Minhāj al-Ṭālibīn. Cairo: Muṣṭafā al-Bābī al-Ḥalabī, 1956.

Al-Qaraḍāwī, Yūsuf, *Al-Madkhal li Dirāsat al-Sharīʿah al-Islāmiyyah*. Cairo: Maktabah Wahba, 1991.

al-Qarāfī (19th century author), Shihāb al-Dīn Abū al-ʿAbbās al-Ṣanhājī, *Al-Furūq*. Beirut: ʿĀlam al-Kutub, n.d.

al-Qurṭubī (b. 656 AH/1258 CE, Spain), Abū ʿAbd Allāh Muḥammad al-Anṣārī, *al-Jāmiʿ li Aḥkām al-Qur'ān*. Beirut: Dār Iḥyā' al-Turāth al-ʿArabī, 1965. 20 vols.

al-Ramlī (b. 957 AH / 1550 CE, Cairo), Shams al-Dīn Muḥammad ibn Aḥmad ibn al-Shihāb, *Nihāyah al-Muḥtāj ilā Sharḥ al-Minhāj*. Cairo: Maṭbaʿah Muṣṭafā al-Bābī al-Ḥalabī, 1386 AH.

al-Rāzī (b. 666 AH / 1268 CE, Iran), Muḥammad ibn Abī Bakr ibn ʿAbd al-Qādir, *Mukhtār al-Ṣiḥāḥ*. 1st edn. Beirut: Dār al-Kitāb al-ʿArabī, 1967.

Ṣāliḥ, Sāʿad Ibrāhīm, *ʿAlāqat al-Ābā' bi al-Abnā' fī al-Shariʿah al-Islāmiyyah: Dirāsah Fiqhiyyah Muqāranah*. [University dissertation] Jeddah: Dār Tihāmah li al-Nashr, 1981.

al-Ṣanʿānī (d. 1182 AH / 1768 CE), Muḥammad ibn Ismāʿīl, *Subul al-Salām Sharḥ Bulūgh al-Marām*, Cairo: Maṭbaʿah al-Imām, n.d.

al-Sanhūrī, ʿAbd al-Razzāq, *al-Wasīṭ fī Sharḥ al-Qānūn al-Madanī*. Cairo: Dār al-Nashr li al-Jāmiʿāt, 1956.

al-Sarakhasī (b. 448 AH / 1056 CE, Bukhara), Muḥammad ibn Aḥmad ibn Abī Sahl, *al-Mabsūṭ*. 1st edn. Cairo: Maṭbaʿah al-Saʿādah, 1320 AH. 30 vols.

al-Shāfiʿī (d. 204 AH / 820 CE, Egypt), Abū ʿAbd Allāh Muḥammad ibn Idrīs, *al-Risālah*. (Ed. Muḥammad Aḥmad Shākir). Cairo: Dār al-Turāth, 1973.

——*al-Umm*. (Margins: *Mukhtaṣar al-Muzanī*). Cairo: Maṭbaʿah Būlāq, 1321 AH. 7 vols.

al-Sharbīnī (b. 977 AH / 1570 CE, Egypt), Muḥammad ibn Aḥmad, *Mughnī al-Muḥtāj fī Maʿrifah Maʿānī Alfāẓ al-Minhāj*. Cairo: Maṭbaʿah Muṣṭafā al-Bābī al-Ḥalabī, 1377 AH. 4 vols.

al-Shawkānī (b. 1205 AH / 1834 CE, Yemen), Muḥammad ibn ʿAlī, *Nayl al-Awṭār (Sharḥ Muntahā al-Akhbār li ʿAbd al-Salām ibn Taymiyyah)*. Cairo: Maṭbaʿah al-Ḥalabī, n.d.

al-Shaykh Mubārak, Qays ibn Muḥammad, *al-Tadāwī wa al-Mas'ūliyyah al-Ṭib-*

biyyah fī al-Sharīʿah al-Islāmiyyah. Damascus: Maktabah al-Fārābī, 1991.

al-Ṭaḥṭāwī (d. 321 AH / 933 CE, Cairo), Aḥmad ibn Muḥammad ibn Ismāʿīl, *Ḥāshiyah al-Ṭaḥṭāwī ʿalā al-Durr al-Mukhtār*. Cairo: al-Maṭbaʿah al-ʿĀmirah, 1238 AH.

al-Ṭarābulsī (b. 1032 AH / 1623 CE, Syria), ʿAlā' al-Dīn Abū al-Ḥasan ʿAlī ibn Khalīl al-Ḥanafī, *Muʿīn al-Ḥukkām fi-mā Yataradad bayn al-Khaṣmayn min al-Aḥkām*. 2nd edn. Cairo: Maṭbaʿah Muṣṭafā al-Bābī al-Ḥalabī, 1973.

ʿUways, ʿAbd al-Ḥalīm, *al-Ḥudūd fī al-Sharīʿah al-Islāmiyyah*. Jeddah: Manshūrāt al-Sharq al-Awsaṭ, n.d.

al-Wanshirīsī (b. 914 AH / 1508 CE, Morocco), Abū al-ʿAbbās Aḥmad ibn Yaḥyā, *al-Miʿyār al-Muʿrib wa al-Jamiʿa al-Mughrib ʿan Fatāwā ʿUlamā' Afrīqyah wa al-Maghrib*. Beirut: Dār al-Gharb al-Islāmī, 1981. 13 vols.

al-Zarkashī (b. 794 AH / 1392 CE, Cairo), *al-Manthūr min al-Qawāʿid*. (Ed. Dr. Taysīr Fā'iq Aḥmad Maḥmūd). Kuwait: Maṭbaʿah Mu'assassah al-Fulayj li al-Ṭibāʿah wa al-Nashr, 1882. 3 vols.

al-Zarqā, al-Shaykh Aḥmad ibn Muḥammad, *Sharḥ al-Qawāʿid al-Fiqhiyyah*. (Revised by ʿAbd al-Sattār Abū Ghudah). Beirut: Dār al-Gharb al-Islāmī, 1403 AH.

al-Zaylāʿī (b. 743 AH / 1343 CE, Cairo), Fakhr al-Dīn ʿUthmān ibn ʿAlī, *Tabayyun al-Ḥaqā'iq Sharḥ Kanz al-Daqā'iq*. Cairo: Maṭbaʿah Būlāq, 1315 AH.

al-Zurqānī (b. 1099 AH / 1688 CE, Cairo), ʿAbd al-Bāqī ibn Yūsuf, *Sharḥ al-Zarqānī ʿalā Mukhtaṣar al-Khalīl*. (In the margin of *Ḥāshiyah al-Bunānī)*. Cairo: Maṭbaʿah Muḥammad Afandī Muṣṭafā, n.d. 8 vols.

ENGLISH WORKS

'American Psychiatric Association Statement on the Insanity Defense', *American Journal of Psychiatry*, vol. 140 (1983), p.6.

Applebaum, P. S., 'Standards for Civil Commitment: A Critical Review of Empirical Research', *International Journal of Law and Psychiatry*, 7 (1984), pp.133–44.

Applebaum, P. S. and Gutheil, T. G., *Clinical Handbook of Psychiatry and the Law*. New York: McGraw-Hill Book Co., 1991.

Burszatajn, H., et al., '*Parens Patriae* Consideration in Commitment Procedures'

Psychiatry Quarterly, 59:3 (Fall 1988).

Cleveland, S., Mulvey, E. P., Applebaum, P. S., et al., 'Do Dangerousness-Oriented Commitment Laws Restrict Hospitalization of Patients Who Need Treatment? A Test', *Hospital and Community Psychiatry*, 40 (1989).

Dawidoff, D., 'Some Suggestions to Psychiatrists for Avoiding Legal Jeopardy', *Archives General Psychiatry*, 29:5 (Nov.1973).

Dobson, J., *Raising Children*. Wheaton, Ill.: Tyndale House Publishing, 1982.

Goldstein, R. L. and Rotter, M., 'The Psychiatrist's Guide to Right and Wrong: Judicial Standards of Wrongfulness since McNaughton', in *Bulletin of the Academy of Psychiatry and the Law*, 16:4 (1988).

Helfer, R. E. and Kempe, R. S., *The Battered Child*. 4th edn. University of Chicago Press: Chicago, 1987.

Hiday, V. A., et al., 'Interpeting the Effectiveness of Involuntory Outpatient Commitment: A Conceptual Model', *Bulletin of the Academy of Psychiatry and the Law*, 25:1 (1997).

Kattan, H., 'Child Abuse in Saudi Arabia: Report on Ten Cases', *Annals of Saudi Medicine*, 1994, vol.14.

Mills, M. J., Sullivan G., and Eth, S., 'Protecting Third Parties: A Decade after Tarasoff', *American Journal of Psychiatry*, 144:1 (Jan. 1987).

Resnick, P. J. 'The Psychiatrist in Court' in Cavenar Jr., J. O. (ed.) *Psychiatry*, Philadelphia: Lippincotti, 1989.

Rosner, R., *Principles and Practise of Forensic Psychiatry* (New York: Chapman & Hall, 1996).

Sadoff, R. L., *Forensic Psychiatry: A Practical Guide for Lawyers and Psychiatrists*. Springfield Ill.: Charles C. Thomas, 1988.

Shields, N. M., McCall, G. J., and Hanneke, C. R., 'Patterns of Family and Non-family Violence', *Violence and Victims*, 3 (1988).

Simon, R. I. (ed.), *Clinical Psychiatry and the Law*. 2nd edn. Washington DC: American Psychiatric Press, 1992.

Stone, A. A., Law, *Psychiatry and Morality*. Washington DC: American Psychiatric Press, 1984.

Stromberg, C. D. and Stone, A. A., 'A Model State Law on Civil Commitment of the Mentally Ill' in R. Rosner (ed.), *Principles and Practice of Forensic Psychiatry*, New York: Chapman & Hall, 1996.

Tighe, J. A., 'Francis Wharton and the Nineteenth-Century Insanity Defense: The Origins of a Reform Tradition', *American Journal of Legal History*, 27 (1983).

Walker, N., *Crime and Insanity in England*. Vol. 1: *The Historical Perspective*. Edinburgh: Edinburgh University Press, 1968.

INDEX